IF IT AIN'T
BROKE—BREAK IT!

IF IT AIN'T BROKE—BREAK IT!

A Document for Both Liberals and Conservatives

by Lois and Don Smith

iUniverse, Inc.

New York Lincoln Shanghai

IF IT AIN'T BROKE—BREAK IT!
A Document for Both Liberals and Conservatives

iUniverse, Inc.

For information address:
iUniverse, Inc.
2021 Pine Lake Road, Suite 100
Lincoln, NE 68512
www.iuniverse.com

ISBN: 0-595-27534-6

Printed in the United States of America

Contents

INTRODUCTION

Three entirely new Concepts (The Triad) are described in this book:

1. End all Federal Personal and Corporate Income Taxes, FICA, and Estate Taxes. Replace with a simple and uniform OTT (Over The Threshold) Fee on all business organizations for services rendered by the Federal government. (Detailed in Chapter 2)

2. End all current Federal Entitlement Programs including Social Security, Welfare, Food Stamps, Public Housing, College Loans, Farm and Corporate Subsidies and Grants to the States. Replace with one simple and uniform Citizen's Dividend. (Detailed in Chapter 3)

3. Privatize Universal Health Care through a single-payer system that preserves individual choice and the profit system of doctor and hospital. (Detailed in Chapter 4)

◆　　　◆　　　◆

And, four premises are honored in this book:

1. That enhancement of Constitutional liberties, economic security and entrepreneurial opportunity works for all of us, and that a smaller less-intrusive Federal government also works better for all of us.

2. That Capitalism and free-markets are the best way to produce new wealth.

3. That Common Sense works! (It tells us that our Nation is an interdependent community; that every citizen in his daily life contributes to the welfare of all of us, and that I'm better off if my neighbor is secure.)

4. That our Nation is a moral nation, is sound, and is on the threshold of its greatest century.

◆　　◆　　◆

This book is necessary because for the last half-century there have been few articulate, vital and podium-pounding spokesmen for real people—that broad centrist coalition of ordinary citizens who raise families, play by the rules, and go to work every day—the beating heart of America. Our major political parties are AWOL on the job of simply making our Nation a better place to live. They are devoid of imagination. So, by default, the job has been left to 'ordinary citizens' who have something to say about who we are and where we're going.

The people we meet and talk to in senior centers, in colleges, in high schools, in coffee shops, on the street, and on airline flights—Democrats, Republicans, Greens, religious folks, agnostics, atheists—are not wild-eyed partisans or steaming ideologues. But they're angry! Angry because they're convinced that politicians of both stripes, in connivance with the media, are in an unholy alliance only to seek election, or re-election, on the one hand, or to sell time and newspapers on the other. The politicians and the media have clearly forgotten that their real 'day job' is to help make America better.

◆　　◆　　◆

"A government that robs Peter to pay Paul can always depend on the support of Paul"

—George Bernard Shaw

Lois and I are not 'compleat libertarians', but we're close enough to their philosophy of individual freedom so that the 'morality' of '...robbing Peter to pay Paul...' bothers us a great deal. Here's our struggle:

On the one hand, It *is* 'morally wrong' to take money from one person by threat of force to give to another person. (Even Christ himself never advocated that.) Yet this what all governments (both liberal and conservative) do to one degree or another. This is the way we live now, and the way people have lived since governments were invented. We know that <u>our</u> government commits this 'moral wrong' every day; yet we stay here to live and raise our families and we validate our government at the ballot box every two to four years.

<u>On the other hand</u>, we've decided to build here a Nation. By definition, half the population of this Nation is below average in capability, intelligence, creativity and drive. We're a Nation of laws; we don't believe in brute animal force to settle disputes or determine who gets what. The upper half will always make the laws and possess the guns to keep order. Therefore, those in the upper half will always wield the power to determine the fortunes of the lower half. We all like the Capitalist system for producing wealth; it's unequaled in efficiency for doing exactly that. Can we depend on an unfettered and unregulated capitalist system to let just enough wealth trickle down to keep the workers alive and healthy?

So, the questions become:

A. What kind of a Nation do we want? Every man for himself, and the devil take the hindmost? Or some tiny enforced (therefore 'immoral') sharing to produce some small degree of leveling to make life a little better for those at the bottom.

B. Should we cross that 'moral boundary' to produce more harmony and more economic output. (We decided almost 200 years ago that it was OK to take money from rich property owners to build and maintain public schools for the poor so we could have a more productive work force. That worked; everybody's better off than they were two centuries ago. And, of course, FDR began an immense 'share-the-wealth' program 70 years ago. That worked, too. Our Nation has seen an incredible increase in wealth, power, influence and standard of living since then. We have millionaires, billionaires, Mercedes, yachts, airplanes, grand estates and super-computers running out of our ears. And that's after fighting WWII and several other wars since then that have sapped huge amounts of our treasure.)

C. In a complex and interdependent industrial and post-industrial society, can anyone say, honestly, that *all* the money he earns is his because no one helped him earn it. (Realize that we count on the children of the poor to defend the shores and combat crime and put out fires and clean the hotel rooms and sweep the streets and pick up the trash so we can all live a comfortable, clean, productive and tranquil life.)

D. Can we resolve the supposed economic problems of the less capable by simply ignoring them? Or do they *have* problems; or do we care? Can't we always depend on the individual and unforced charity, largess or nobless oblige' of the smarter and more capable people to ease the burdens of the poor.

ARE WE A GREAT NATION? CAN WE DO BETTER?

PART I

DEADLY SERIOUS—
To Build a New Nation

1

The TRIAD

The Triad of Concepts described in this book are doable. These three 'ideas' are magnetic in their appeal, and they'll improve our National life...and our personal lives.... beyond any political ideas proposed in recent times. The catch is that it'll take political courage to introduce them into the public debate.

Do we have any people with courage and vision in the political arena? Our President, George W. Bush, has the clout, the stamina and the public support to change our Nation.

But, does he have the vision and the will?

WHERE ARE THE GIANTS?

Political courage is a rare commodity these days. We don't see any 'giants' on the scene. We don't see any FDR's, Truman's, Marshall's, Eisenhower's, Taft's, Vandenburg's, LBJ's, Morse's, Humphrey's, Nixon's, Carter's, or Reagan's on the scene in 2003.

But, perhaps somewhere in that current assemblage of 535 Congresspersons, or perhaps somewhere in the Executive Branch, or somewhere in the heart and soul of our Nation we can find a champion; *all* new ideas need a champion. It will take imagination, because these three things that you'll read about from here on have never been done before anywhere; but isn't 'imagination' an American pride.

Imagine a Nation with no personal Federal Tax Returns to file, and no regressive FICA Tax. A Nation that will save 600,000,000 man-hours of wasted time and $30 billion by ending Personal and Corporate Income Taxes altogether. Imagine a Nation with the stress, clutter, invasive, corrupting, and stifling effect of the

Income Tax....Gone! And all other Federal Taxes (Estate, Inheritance, Unemployment Compensation...............) Gone!

Imagine a Nation with no selective, corrupting and wasteful Entitlement Programs, and with no involuntary poverty. A Nation that will save 200,000,000 man-hours and about $10 billion of bureaucratic wasted effort. A Nation where the economy will bubble with a sustained level of prosperity, with a new surge of entrepreneurialism, with no punishment of success; and where families will find help and encouragement to stay together. A Nation where every *citizen* will share in the general prosperity in addition to the personal earnings for his own particular skill, talents and energy.

Imagine a Nation which recognizes that defense of a citizen's health is equal in importance to the defense of our borders. Without question or argument, 'National Defense' must include 'health defense'. How can one be in favor of a 'Star Wars' missile defense system, which is designed to protect the health and life of every citizen, but oppose all forms of Universal Health Care which is designed to do exactly the same thing?

Imagine a Nation where medical care returns to the old-fashioned successful mode of fee-for-service, and where doctors, nurses, technicians and hospitals are once again care-givers and not financial agents for unnecessary layers of bureaucracy. Imagine a Nation with first-quality Health Care immediately available to every citizen regardless of means or circumstances.

AS A GREAT NATION, WE CAN DO IT!

2

New Concept #1
End All Federal Taxes!

Here's what we're proposing:

Replace all Federal taxes—Income Taxes (both Personal and Corporate), FICA, Estate Taxes, Inheritance Taxes, Unemployment Compensation—with a small (5%) Optional 'Pass-through' **O**ver **T**he **T**hreshold (**OTT**) F̲e̲e̲ on all monies or equivalent received by every business[1].

---

1. Two things are important to note here:
    1. This **OTT** Fee, which, optionally, can be passed directly through to the customer or client, applies to *all* monies (or equivalent) coming in to a business entity (Retail Sales, Wholesale Sales, Bank Deposits, Credit Card Issuers, Brokerage Accounts, Country Club Memberships, Professional Fees, Loans, etc.) This feature assures that the revenue burden of government is shared evenly and p̲r̲o̲p̲o̲r̲t̲i̲o̲n̲a̲l̲l̲y̲ by all income levels in direct relation to how they use the services of government, and that the system cannot be tweaked in favor of one group or another. All income, no matter how acquired, is spent, invested or saved. Since domestic banks and brokerage houses will likely waive the OTT Fee to attract large deposits, there will be little incentive to sequester funds in foreign accounts. More money will stay home.
    2. It is hard to overstate the financial advantages to businesses of being shorn of the direct and administrative costs of FICA contributions, employee health care, pension systems, business and employee income tax calculations and compliance, and minimum wage compliance. The **OTT** (and the other two segments of the Triad as described in the next two chapters) by replacing all the present administrative and financial nightmares of business will be an historic boon to business vitality.

5

<u>The Rationale for Establishing a 'Fee' System on Businesses as a Replacement for Income Taxes.</u>

The use of the word 'Fee', and the dropping of the word 'Taxes' is neither accidental nor incidental. Not only are 'Taxes' themselves onerous, the very word 'Tax' carries an negative connotation from the earliest impositions of tribute levied on the common folk by tyrants, emperors, despots and kings. 'Fees', on the other hand, are legitimate payments for services received.

1. Businesses are the organizations and activities that we charter and designate to produce the goods and services we need. Recognizing that the success of businesses is essential to the welfare of the Nation, the body politic, through government, provides for businesses a whole panoply of law services, a stable monetary and banking system, foreign trade assistance, monopoly protection, census information, employee health care and regulated infrastructures of communication, transportation, homeland security and national defense to protect their interests and assure domestic tranquility and a free-flow of commerce. Since the use of government services and the infrastructure is roughly proportional to the number of dollars that flow through a business, the OTT Fee is fair and equitable.

2. By the very nature of business as a money collection and distribution mechanism, it is ideally suited to act as a collection agency for the revenues needed for government operations and initiatives. It's obvious that a simple percentage calculation on the part of 3,000,000 businesses is far more efficient and less costly to the 'body politic' than the intricate and complex calculations required of 3,000,000 businesses *and* 130,000,000 individuals to comply with a 7500-page tax code.

3. It's a truism that any 'tax' or 'fee' on a business enterprise is ultimately borne by the customer, or the shareholder or the employee. But, by explicitly designating the OTT Fee as—'optional pass-through'—, the entire energy and ingenuity of the competitive nature of business is brought to bear so that the burden on any individual business is determinable by that particular business based entirely on competitive circumstances. It is very close to being a voluntary 'tax'. The skill and efficiency of a business in reducing its costs is immediately rewarded, not punished.

The consumer, of course, ultimately 'pays' the Fee, because he's the only one who can. (All revenues which go to sustain government operations are merely diversions of con-

*sumption from individuals to government; we give up buying something so govern-
ment can have part of the money we earn to buy what they need to operate and do
what we ask them to do.)*

Here's the way the OTT will work:

Company A mines ore and sells the ore to a Steel producer (Company B), and
adds a 5% OTT Fee to the bill. (Or Company A may elect, for competitive reasons, to *not*[2] charge Company B the OTT Fee.)

Company B sells Steel to a manufacturer of Tools (Company C), and adds a 5%
OTT Fee to the bill. (Or Company B may elect, for competitive reasons, to
not[2] charge Company C the OTT Fee.)

Company C sells the finished Tools to a Retail Store (Company D), and adds a
5% OTT Fee to the bill. (Or Company C may elect, for competitive reasons, to
not[2] charge Company D the OTT Fee.)

The store (Company D) sells you a Tool and adds a 5% OTT Fee to the bill (Or
the store may elect, for competitive reasons, to *not*[2] charge you the OTT Fee.)

ADVANTAGES OF THE OTT Fee

1. Administration is simple; one neat straightforward percentage calculation, one
monthly mailing or electronic deposit to the United States Treasury.

2. The OTT Fee is a small percentage in each case, which practically eliminates
any incentive to evade or to establish offshore.

3. The genius of the OTT Fee is the explicitness of the competitive tool it hands
to every business; the decision to pass-through or *not* pass-through at any time or
for any circumstance. And, again, the reward for efficiency is full and immediate.

---

2.   Whether any seller (Company A, Company B, Company C or Company D) elects
     to pass-through, or *not* pass-through, the OTT Fee to the buyer, he is still required
     to remit his 5% Fee monthly to the United States Treasury (based on his total sales,
     or receipts of deposits).

4. While it may appear at first glance that the compounding effect of the OTT Fee as a material or product moves through the chain would result in higher prices, this is not the case for two reasons: Every business is spared the present high cost of complying with very complex tax codes and high tax payments; and competition will assure that many times the OTT Fee will not be passed on. (And, of course, you'll have more money in your pocket because there will be *no* Income Tax and *no* FICA withheld from your paycheck.)

5. With the OTT Fee in place replacing both the personal Income Tax and the Estate Tax, there is no limit placed on an individual's accumulation or ultimate distribution of his wealth; there is no 'punishment' of individual success, there is no incentive to move money offshore. For the talented, the energetic, the lucky, the sky's the limit!

Now the frosting on the cake:

1. **600,000,000** man-hours saved every year by the private sector by eliminating complex tax calculations, and by government by ending the IRS as we know it. How much is 600,000,000 manhours? *More* than the man-hours required to build every car and truck, and every toy, built in the USA! *More* than the man-hours required to build 300,000 homes! *More* than the man-hours that would be required to provide annual preventive medical attention to every citizen of the USA!

2. No more personal stress. Each time you buy something, or deposit a check, your tax bill is paid up. No more April 15th, no 1099's, no 1040's, no Quarterly Filings, no Record Keeping, no Bulging Correspondence Files with the IRS about niggling details of your 3-year old Tax Return, no costly Tax Avoidance Schemes, no 401k's, no IRA's, no offshore Tax Havens, no bulky and opaque Tax Booklets, no Depreciation Calculations, no W-2's, or W-4's, no Tax Attorneys, no 1080's, no 668's, no H&R Block, no Tax Preparers.

3. Business will make 'Business' Decisions, not 'Tax' Decisions. This fact alone will lead to more efficient (lower cost) operations, and will keep more money at home and at work, and not idling in offshore 'tax havens'.

4. Every business and every person will pay a share of the cost of government in direct proportion to their use of the 'system'.

5. Revenues will flow into the Treasury in an even stream year-round, allowing greater predictability and lessening the need for borrowing; thus leading to lower interest rates and a more vibrant economy...

CONCLUSIONS For New Concept #1

The replacement of the Income Tax with a new OTT Fee is a Win-Win. There are no losers except the folks who are growing fat on our dime because of the incredible complexities and the corruption potential of the current system. Working people win, businesses win, honest government wins.

The people who will oppose this measure are in two groups: A) The politicians in Washington, because it deprives them of most of their power; and B) The thousands of 'professionals' who make their living by helping the rest of us thread our way through the impossibly complicated Tax Code.

AS A GREAT NATION, WE CAN DO BETTER!

3

New Concept #2
End all present Entitlements;
Establish a CITIZEN'S
DIVIDEND (CD)!

<u>Here's what we're proposing:</u>

End all present Entitlement Programs, Federal Minimum Wage Laws and Grants to the States. Replace with a Citizen's Dividend of **$175**/mo. to every citizen beginning at age 13; becoming **$350**/mo. @ age 18; and doubling to **$700**/mo. @ age 67. Not taxable by the States, and exempt from legal judgments. Payable to a named beneficiary till age 67 in the event of imprisonment or premature death after age 13.

<u>Here's how and why it will work:</u>

Paid only to Citizens, and indexed annually to the GDP. Money to be deposited monthly (electronically) in an account at a bank or other institution of the recipients choice. Ended would be all Farm Subsidies, Food Stamps, Welfare, Corporate Subsidies, Social Security, Public Housing, Grants to the States, etc. Administered through the present efficient Social Security system. Special 'hardship cases', 'necessary' Farm Subsidies and Minimum Wage Laws would be covered by the States at their discretion.

The current outlay for all Entitlement Programs and Grants to the States is about $1.2 trillion/yr. The outlay from the Treasury for the **CD** program described above is about $1.2 trillion/yr.; therefore, no net new cost to the Nation.

Eligibility for the **CD** is verified by proof of citizenship, and by simply formally requesting the payment; and is renewed each year at the local postoffice by re-registering. We estimate that 5% to 10% of those eligible will not request the payment for personal reasons; just as many well-to-do now do not choose to take Social Security payments, and many others, less well-to-do, donate hundreds of millions of dollars every year to the Federal Government.

By ending the FICA under New Concept #1, *and* with the establishment of the **CD,** we have automatically 'privatized Social Security'. Every citizen will now have the means to buy more goods and services. The extra money spent will automatically provide extra profit (investment capital) to those companies who provide the most desirable product for the consumer and are thus most likely to succeed and grow, thus insuring their growth and their ability to throw off future dollars for maintenance and growth of the **CD** program, which is linked to the GDP. Every consumer plays the part of an investor in the companies whose product or service he favors. Additionally, the **CD** itself becomes a source of funds by which every individual who so chooses has the ability to directly invest in companies or securities of his choice to enhance his retirement fund.

There are a few particularly interesting items about the **CD:**
1. If the **CD** for a minor is retained in a Savings Account until age 18, the accumulated amount, with normal interest compounded, would be about $12,000. A nice start for college or for life.

2. The **CD** total for a retired couple is less than the present Social Security yields, but there are two caveats:

A. Savings of only $100/month of the CD beginning at age 25, and at a nominal 6% rate of interest, will become over $216,000 at age 67. A married couple, on that basis, would have a nest egg of over $432,000 at age 67, together with a CD income of $1400/mo. for life.

B. All present retirees under the Social Security system would continue to be covered as they are now. All present workers covered under the current Social Security system would be guaranteed the same amount at retirement as they are now scheduled.

3. The **CD** will bring stability to the economy. A steady and predictable flow of cash into the Treasury and back to individuals will reduce the need for government borrowing and will create a constant spending stream on the part of consumers. Investments will be guided by how consumers choose to spend their

money. The extra cash and the assurance of bottom-line income in consumers hands will create new opportunities of entrepreneurialism for ordinary creative people who would otherwise be unwilling or unable to take risks.

4. The **CD** is not another 'welfare' idea; rather it's a means of reducing the cost of government, of stabilizing the economy, and of creating an element of security and stability for family life and responsible parenthood.

Recognizing that the **CD** could be considered by many to be a radical idea, and certainly at first reading may be offensive to Conservative philosophy, it seems a good time to hark back in our history to writings by one of our revolutionary for-bears, Thomas Paine. Paine was fascinated by the Principles of Government, and was instrumental in stirring up support for our War for Independence through his widely distributed leaflet, 'Common Sense' and his other provocative writings.

Paine wrote several essays, pamphlets, dissertations and books dealing with the relationship between people and their government. His topics ranged from Slavery to God to Dreams and to the Rights of Man.

One of his essays, 'Agrarian Justice', deals with the intriguing, and self-evident, idea that the real progress of mankind began with cultivated agriculture which necessarily led to permanence of residence and to the concepts of land ownership and private property rights. This ineluctably led Paine to the realization that though the establishment of private land ownership was immensely beneficial to the whole of mankind because it enabled vastly increased production of food-stuffs, it denied to all future generations their 'birthright' to a piece of the whole land that God had created. (As Paine pointed out, God didn't establish a land office to parcel out land; Man did.) Let's read what Paine wrote:

Paraphrasing from Thomas Paine—

In the beginning there was no land office established by the creator that parceled out the land to various owners in perpetuity. Since there was much land and few people, there was always new land available for each person born on which to create his own sustenance and value. With cultivation and industrialization, users of various parcels of land greatly increased the value of that land. This introduced the entirely proper concept of 'landed property'

Then quoting directly from Thomas Paine in 'Agrarian Justice'—

"It is only by tracing things to their origin that we can gain rightful ideas of them, and it is by gaining such ideas that we discover the boundary that divides right from wrong,————while, therefore, I advocate the right, of all those who [have been dispossessed] of their natural inheritance by the introduction of 'landed property', I equally defend the right of the possessor to [that wealth which he has created over and above the value of the land.]"

"Cultivation [and Industrialization] are the great improvements that were made by human invention. But the landed monopoly that began with it————has dispossessed [the new] inhabitants of every nation of their natural inheritance [that being land itself].

"In advocating the case of persons thus dispossessed, it is a right, and not a charity, that I am pleading for. But it is that kind of right that could not be brought forwards till heaven had opened the way by a revolution in the system of government. Let us, then do honor to revolutions by justice, and give currency to their principles by blessings.

"Having thus, in a few words, opened the merits of the case, I shall now proceed to the plan I have to propose, which is:

"To create a National Fund, out of which there shall be paid to every [citizen], when arrived at the age of 21 years, the sum of 15 pounds sterling, as a compensation, in part, for the loss of his or her natural inheritance, by the introduction of the system of landed property. And also the sum of ten pounds per annum, during life to every [citizen] now living of the age of 50 years, and to all others as they shall arrive at that age."

Note: Bracketed portions are the Author's updating of the language but are faithful to the intent of Paine.

Although the prescience of Paine was a part of our concluding that the principle of the Citizen's Dividend was valid, there's more. Simple logic tells us that no man in a complex and well-governed industrial society achieves a high standard of living or accumulates wealth entirely on his own. He is, in a sense, standing on the shoulders of those who came before; some of whom worked hard at building and maintaining the infrastructure, and others who paid the maximum sacrifice at Gettysburg or the Argonne, or who waded into hell on the beaches of Normandy or Iwo Jima, or who climbed Pork Chop Hill or at the Chosin Resevoir, or Ia Drang or Que Sahn.

Capitalism and the Free-market succeed brilliantly at their primary job of creating wealth, and ought not be tampered with; but the teeter-totter[1] effect often amplifies the differences in extractions from the output, and masks the contributions of the lower paid among us to the general welfare and to the accumulation of wealth by others.

CONCLUSIONS For New Concept #2

Granted; it is indeed a bold suggestion that every citizen has a claim to a share of both the wealth of the natural 'commons' and the humanly-created wealth of our Nation. Bold, perhaps, but neither unthinkable nor unreasonable.

It is, perhaps, too easy for us in our comfort and luxury to forget that over the last 215 years, millions of Americans have made the supreme sacrifice of their life or the soundness of their body to enable the rest of us to live out our lives as we choose. Those who didn't die put their life on the line, and on hold, for the rest of us. And, among us now are millions of men and women who must, and will, answer the call to defend this Nation if the need arises.

Less threatened with death or bodily harm, perhaps, are the millions of people who labor every day for small pay to keep our world clean, comfortable and livable. These are the folks who clean the hotel rooms, who pick the fruit and harvest the vegetables, who drive the trucks, who teach our kids, who fight crime and fires, who build and fix the roads, who repair our cars and our appliances, or who work in the hot sun or the freezing cold to repair the electric lines. These hard-working people build and repair the very infrastructure that enables those of us who design, who plan, who write, who risk, who talk, who work in air-conditioned offices to make our dreams come true. These same hard-working folks don't have the time or the resources to gain access to their representatives for special consideration, yet they contribute greatly. We want them to have a direct and tangible stake in our National success.

---

1.   Balance a teeter-totter to a perfect horizontal with 100 pounds at each end; add 1 pound to one end (1%), and that end hits the ground.

Yes, in our free-market capitalist economy, they are compensated according to the willingness of the employer, or according to the leverage they can bring to bear from collective bargaining. But their innate capabilities and their station in life put them at a disadvantage when challenging real power for a decent share of the Nation's output. So, who can say that they are properly compensated for their labors? As on a see-saw, a tiny imbalance of power can cause a hugely disproportionate and unseemly disparity in outcomes and incomes.

AS A GREAT NATION, WE CAN DO BETTER!

The **CD** will serve as a small adjustment for the damaging wrinkles that inevitably occur in the smooth fabric of a well-disciplined free-market economy. And by indexing this dividend to the GDP, each citizen will have a 'direct and tangible' stake in the National progress. We all become shareholders in the United States of America, vitally interested in our National financial success, and cheerleaders for those among us who create new sources of wealth or increases in productivity. We will end the scourge of 'class envy'.

Beyond the moral underpinning of the case for a **CD** are four pragmatic imperatives; to wit:

1. Since the constant and uninterruptible flow of dollars to every family will be added to any 'earned' income rather than being diminished by those earnings, the incentive to work, to earn and to create new ideas will be stronger than ever. (All current 'welfare', 'subsidy' and Earned Income Tax Credit payments are automatically reduced if additional income is earned; thus proving to be a dis-incentive to work and earn.)

2. Marriage and the family will be solidly encouraged. With a solid base of income for each member, families will be encouraged to invest in the future. The financial underpinning provided by the **CD** will encourage families to stay together under trying circumstances rather than break apart in hopelessness. The 'bottom line' of income will encourage entrepreneurship since it will provide more capital for savings, and failure will be less disastrous. And, if failure is avoided, then the **CD** income will be the icing on the cake of success.

3. The steady and uninterruptible infusion of dollars into the income stream of *all* of the Nation's families will even out the vagaries of retail sales which represent 1/3 of the GDP. There will be a stabilization of the ability to purchase a new

home, a new car or a new refrigerator, or simply to go to a movie, or go on a trip more often.

4. Of that monthly flow of dollars into the savings institutions, a large percentage will remain in the accounts and be available to the institutions as lending capital, thus creating a stable and lower interest rate structure and making possible the buying and building of new homes for more people.

Economic benefits will flow to all levels of income from these 4 'pragmatic imperatives', thus enriching and securing the Nation.

There won't be an inflationary effect of **CD's** because there is no 'new' money being added to the total in circulation. All that's being augmented is constancy and wider distribution; both of which are stabilizing and prosperity-inducing in their effect.

One of the wiser virtues of the **CD** is that it allows the cessation of all of the cumbersome, costly, complex and inherently unfair maze of programs of Subsidies, Welfare, Food Stamps, Unemployment Compensation, Social Security and Grants to the States. Thus, a full 20% of the Federal Bureaucracy is rendered unneeded. A caveat here is that there may need to be a gradual transfer of Farm Subsidy responsibility from the Federal Government to the States because subsidies have been embedded in the farm economy for so long that they have distorted the *acreage-cost-price* balance. Too many farmers are growing too much food and need price supports. In time, and with help from the individual States to their own farmers, the adjustment to economic realities can be made without undue hardship.

Federal Aid to Education, and Grants to the States can be studied in a new light because a stream of 'Federal' money (**CD's**) will be flowing to the States' citizens in direct proportion to their population, making it possible for the States to manage their affairs through their individual tax structures without the obvious subterfuge of claiming 'Federal' money as though 'Federal' money was manufactured from some extra-planetary source other than their own taxpayers.

Example: In 2002, an 'Education Bill' was passed in the Congress and signed into law. This bill authorized $20B for 2002 to go to the various States for improving educational standards. Presumably, California (12% of the Nation's population) will receive about $2.4B of this money. (Of course the fraud is evident here in the fact that the $2.4B came from California in the first place, Washington only laundered the money; for a steep price.) Under the **CD** program, California citizens would receive about $60B of extra discretionary income; quite sufficient to pay for complying with the new 'standards' on their own. A similar example to this can be constructed for the numerous 'Grants to the States' program that Congress authorizes each year.

Once **CD** money begins to flow to individuals in the States, the States will, with their normal financial resources, and with the reductions in their case loads, be able resolve any 'hardship' cases of welfare or subsidies within their own jurisdiction. We can once again begin to assert 'States' Responsibilities' coincident with the cry for 'States' Rights'.

AS A GREAT NATION, WE CAN DO BETTER!

4

New Concept #3
PRIVATIZED SINGLE-PAYER UNIVERSAL HEALTH CARE!

Here's what we're proposing:

A Single-payer Universal Health Care (**SUHC**) program, funded by an OTT Fee of 3% on the gross revenues of every business enterprise, with no government involvement except as the collection agency, that will insure basic health care for every American citizen. Since business is the most direct beneficiary of a strong and healthy work force, the idea of business sharing the cost burdens with users stands the test of logic.

SUHC will bear no resemblance to the complicated, expensive and sub-par National Health Care or 'Socialized Medicine' programs of other countries. It will be USA born-and-bred and will be well-administered by the medical profession, *not* by government.

Here's why and how it will work.

Why are we bringing up Universal Health Care again? Because it's time. Time for a Declaration of War! The defense of the health and vitality of every citizen against foreign bacterial and viral invaders, and against the ravages of debilitating disease and injury, is every bit as pertinent, important and Constitutional as the defense of our shores and borders against foreign human invaders or terrorists. Our Nation is not simply geography; it is us, we the people.

Would we vote to abandon a strong Defense Department and leave the military defense of our Nation to a hodge-podge of competing interests of Defense Maintenance Organizations, Public Agencies, Insurance Companies and military professionals?

Why Universal Health Care? Because the health of every citizen of our Nation is a common concern. Centuries ago, we realized that universal 'Public' Education, 'Public' Libraries, 'Public' Police Departments, 'Public' Fire Departments and 'Public' Parks and, indeed, a 'Public' Military were important to the general welfare. We recognized that universal education, the wide dissemination of knowledge and information, the protection of life and property, and open space and recreation are important to the increasing prosperity, the happiness and the very soundness of our Nation. Those leaders at that time saw beyond the narrowly-interpreted strictures of the Constitution to its goal which was to preserve individual freedom, but at the same time use the power of community in addition to individual effort to enhance life. They believed the phrase "—general welfare—" in the Constitution was a mandate that could, through the reasonable process of a representative-type democracy, allow some small infringement on the wealth or earnings (not the personal 'unalienable' rights) of all of us in order to achieve a broad National goal that stands to benefit every citizen in the longer run of time. A commitment to Public Health Care is a commitment to national security and is not unlike the commitment to public education or to the exploration of space.

The Founders were practical men. It's logical to assume that they knew intuitively that the Nation they were chartering would grow and develop; new ideas and new technologies were emerging even as they were meeting. They would have known that many of the words they were using to describe their thoughts and their instincts would have to be re-interpreted in the lights of new generations, and they would have known that those 're-interpretations' would cause much political and social strife. They provided for amendments, certainly, but they also would have known that there would be many issues arise that would fall short of requiring or deserving of the process of amendment; thus the provision in the Constitution for a Congress and a Supreme Court.

Our Nation has believed in Universal Public Education for over 200 years. There's never been any serious challenge to the concept that every child is guaranteed an education at public expense for grades K-12. While some think the system is flawed and is failing to produce excellence, the fact remains that the product of this educational system, the men and women who have nurtured and developed this Nation to presently being the top of the world in technical excellence, in prosperity, and in steadfastly adhering to democratic principles and the principle of justice under the law are almost entirely the product of our Public Education system. It works!

The notion that the health of every citizen is as vital as education, and is a reasonable burden for the public at large to share because of its importance to the general welfare, is not a radical one.

The health of every citizen is important to all of us. Not only is the spread of infectious disease a constant and universal concern, but the *economic* consequences of ordinary every-day sickness, and of Alzheimers, Parkinson's, Cancer and Heart/Lung disease (to say nothing of the personal tragedies) impact all of our lives. The well-to-do have every bit as much at stake, and as much at risk, as you and I do in the health and soundness of every citizen. Short of war or foreign invasion, there is no more important battle that our Nation wages than the struggle against ill health, disease and infirmity. It's a 'common concern', certainly on at least the same level and as Constitutionally sound as defending the Nation against foreign enemies.

There is, in fact, as much justification for mounting a comprehensive National program to defend every citizen's body and mind against viral or bacterial invasion, or organic malfunction, as there is to defend that citizen's life and property against an foreign invader of our shores or borders. It's appalling, it's unpatriotic and it's un-Christian to think otherwise.

Every baby born among us is an asset for the future welfare of the Nation and for our personal welfare; it would be folly to allow that asset to waste because of inadequate or unaffordable health care. If we're conscious of what's at stake for that baby, and for our own future as older people, we really have no choice. We must assure that every citizen, regardless of means, has at his disposal the finest of health care systems at the lowest of overall cost. And it's only logical that that cost be shared by every one of us. None of us knows when the need for that system will strike home to us or our loved ones, nor do we know what our ability to pay will be at that time. It's only sensible that the entire Nation be considered one giant pool of risk, and that we maintain a standing army to meet that risk.

Fortunately, the 'army' that will protect our health and well-being is already in being and is well equipped—the medical care profession of administrators, doctors, nurses, clinics and hospitals. All they need is to be freed of the economic and personal burdens of excessive oversight and 'cost containment'. Our doctors and medical treatment professionals can be trusted; they just need to be liberated from excessive bureaucracy and paperwork and allowed to practice medicine. And they need to be assured of high incomes proportionate to their training and value to the rest of us.

Because we have a market-driven system of production of hi-tech equipment and a combined private and government-sponsored drug and medical research program, we have achieved technological excellence in our level of medical care possibilities. But the delivery system is a costly, stuttering and incomplete patchwork that misses many people at many times in their life and does not encourage preventive medical attention. And the delivery system is laden with the costly financial and paperwork overhead of HMO's, Doctor's Groups, and Insurance Companies that serve no economic function, but act merely as 'gatekeepers'—often to the detriment of the patient who needs preventive or curative help NOW!

AS A GREAT NATION, WE CAN DO BETTER!

◆   ◆   ◆

Fee-for-service and the direct relationship between the doctor of choice and the patient worked for 150 years; it still works. Our proposal here is simply that we cover all medical costs through a single-payer which is funded in its entirety by American business through a simply administered and small competitively-allocated pass-through OTT Fee of 3%. The idea of employer-subsidized health insurance is not radical; employees of most businesses are now covered by one of the myriad of health care plans offered by the various insurance companies and HMO's. But one comprehensive national plan funded by business and consumers, and administered by medical professionals, will save billions in costs while insuring that every American citizen will receive adequate care. The genius of the free-market is that the cost burden will be distributed throughout the business chains in a shifting, fluid and self-correcting manner depending on the competitive pressures of individual businesses

PRIVATIZE UNIVERSAL HEALTH CARE—HOW? The current total of costs for all medical care in our Nation is about 13% of the GDP, or about One

Trillion dollars This cost is borne by a panoply of individuals, businesses, and various levels of government (Federal, State and Local). In the present patchwork system of delivering medical care, there are several layers of overhead expense in the various HMO's, Insurance Companies and diverse government agencies that regulate the disbursement of the money but contribute nothing to patient care. By eliminating these layers, the actual cost of real health care would be reduced to about 12% of GDP; A reduction in cost of about 10 Billion dollars, representing the release of about 250,000,000 man-hours that can serve patients or engage in other productive pursuits in the general economy. That represents 125,000 people who could then perform useful and needed tasks; either in medicine or in the general work force.

These 125,000 intermediaries now act principally as 'gatekeepers' and masseurs of funds that are paid by the patient or other agency to the doctor or hospital. This 'gatekeeper' function and the delays in payment resulting from needless overhead greatly complicates the essential job of patient care and medical decision-making by both the doctor and the hospital; and can cause, and has caused, serious lapses in proper and timely treatment.

Our corps of medical care personnel (doctors, nurses, technicians and hospital personnel) are highly professional and can, and must, be trusted to make the proper decisions without a bureaucratic financial institution looking over their shoulder.

We must return to the simple and effective method of direct fee-for-service that well served many generations of Americans before the latter half of the 20th Century.

When a health care provider submits a bill for a standard office call (estimated at $30) or other service, it must be co-signed by the patient, after which it will be sent to the single-payer 'pool' that has been funded annually by the business sector, from which the bill will be paid promptly. Bills for costs above the standard fees prescribed by the AMA will be paid for by the patient. Thus the patient will be free to use any care provider of choice since he will be responsible for any costs above the standard fee. Constant computer monitoring of costs in the various regions by the AMA to assure reasonableness will avoid any government interference in health care. Nobody wants 'socialized medicine'.

Government's only responsibility, and only function in the system, is to collect sufficient funds annually through the OTT Fee to cover the cost of basic health care for every citizen. Obviously, a trillion dollars of cost to fund Universal Health Care is a huge number, but it's not a new cost to the Nation as a whole. This same trillion dollars is now being spent directly by individuals for insurance premiums and direct care, and by businesses (in administrative overhead and insurance premiums) and by Local, State and Federal agencies for medical care for indigents and seniors.

For the Nation as a whole, there is no increased cost; in fact there are substantial savings due to decreased overhead. It's a matter of shifting the costs of medical coverage from the current panoply of individuals, businesses, institutions and government agencies entirely to businesses where it will be met through a 3% optional pass-through OTT rate. (Refer back to Chapter 2.) It's the marvel of the free-market system in competitively adjusting to new costs, new savings and new uses for productive labor that will make transition to the new plan immediate and workable.

Adoption of this Universal Health Care plan, with a single-payer, will permit huge reductions in the size and cost of Federal and Local governments through the ending of most of the various health care agencies at all levels of government.

We can, and must, trust the medical profession (both the AMA as an organization, and the doctors and hospitals) to administer this Universal Health Care plan to achieve better and more prompt health care at reduced costs. We want doctors, nurses, hospitals and all health care professionals to be well compensated and regarded with the respect this important profession deserves. And, of course, malpractice awards must carry reasonable caps on pain and suffering.

Because this plan will make life better for medical professionals, we expect their enthusiastic acceptance, and their integrity and diligence to make it work fairly.

We say let's hand them the keys to our new car; and trust them to drive safely.

CONCLUSIONS FOR NEW CONCEPT #3

With a sane and universal health care plan in place, our Nation will take a giant step toward becoming healthier. We can begin a concentrated nationwide effort to inform our citizens of the importance of proper nutrition, exercise and weight control. And through regularized 'free' pre-natal care and preventive medicine for both children and adults, we will forestall many health problems and begin to lower overall health care costs by 1/3 over the next 5-10 years.

PART II

PROVOCATIVE—
Political Philosophy—The
Great Divide

5

CONSERVATIVE v. LIBERAL

CONSERVATISM—

Strident and Unquestioning Nationalism, Strict Interpretation of the Constitution—

Military Supremacy Over Other Nations—

A Fascination With War, Strength and Violence in Problem-solving—

Emphatic About Capitalism and Free-markets; Minimal Regulation by Government—

Personal Economic Freedom

Economic Growth by Tax Cuts and Trickle-down From Topside Investment—

Disciplined Personal Behavior Based Largely on Religious Teachings—

Sharp Delineation of Good and Evil, Emphatic Punishment for Crimes—

Low Taxes—Opposes 'Progressive' Taxation—

Opposes Social Programs and *Redistribution of Income*[1] to Aid Persons—

Emphasizes 'Costs' of Environmental Maintenance and Improvement—

Minimal Government—

Opposes Any Form of Taxpayer-supported Universal Health Care

LIBERALISM—

Continually Questions National Goals; Broad Interpretation of the Constitution—

Not Emphatic on Military Strength—

A Fascination With Compromise and Negotiation in Problem-solving—

Favors Capitalism But With Strong Regulation to Prevent Excesses—

Personal Social Freedom

Economic Growth by Increasing Consumer Purchasing Power—

More Personal Freedom of Behavior; Little Religious Influence, The Golden Rule—

Recognition of Good and Evil, But Always Hope for Redemption—

Favors 'Progressive' Taxation Sufficient to Support Social Programs—

Favors a Degree of *Redistribution of Income*[1] to Improve Life for The Less Capable—

Favors Strong Environmental Protections; Lesser Emphasis on 'Cost'—

A Government Sufficient to Regulate Business and Assure Some Redistribution—

Favors a Reasonable Form of Universal Health Care

The crystalline political issue of all societies is the balance of the primacy of the individual against the perceived needs of the group or state of which that individual is a part. All individuals want freedom of expression and action for them-

---

1.   The issue of 'Redistribution of Income (Wealth)' is an absolutely crucial difference of philosophy between Liberal (Left) and Conservative (Right). It colors all the arguments between Left and Right over economic policy. The critical question hovering over this entire book is this: Can a case be made for using the power of government to interfere to some degree with the natural forces of competition and the free-market in order to add a little flavor and security to the lives of the working poor and the less talented and less capable among us?

selves, and resist coercion from other individuals or from some political body. But all individuals also want security against the natural hazards of life and against harm from other individuals.

It's against this backdrop of conflicting 'wants' that political philosophies are formed and political parties are born and shaped. 'Conservative' political philosophy speaks heavily to the primacy of the individual on economic issues, control by the state on moral issues, and protection of the individual against harm from other individuals. 'Liberal' political philosophy speaks heavily for the rights of the individual in moral issues, but also to the needs of the group or the state to assist the less capable to have a decent life.

Complicating the rather simple delineation described above is the element of religion. In spite of the complete absence of any evidence that there is any 'higher being' or any 'god', most people choose 'faith' as a way of life. For some inexplicable reason, people of Conservative political leanings are far more apt to believe in 'God' and derive their moral guidance from that source, than are Liberals. Conservatives draw much sharper lines between 'good' and 'evil' than do Liberals.

It's true that there is no specific reference in our remarkable Constitution to justify using taxation to take money from one individual, to benefit another specific individual. Technically, that's infringing on the economic liberty of one person in order to benefit another person, by using 'force' or the threat of force, to carry out a charitable task. The Constitution specifically provides for using collected taxes to provide for the 'common defense', for a system of justice, and a for few other specific functions that are to protect and serve us all equally. But our Founders were wise men; the phrase '—general welfare—' as used twice in the Constitution (in the Preamble and in Article 1, Section 8) was not accidental, nor was it a 'slip of the tongue'. Months of deliberation, and intense debate, went into the drafting of the Constitution; every word was parsed for its own meaning, as well as its context. It was apparent to the Founders that the future was unknowable in its details; the first glimmerings of the Industrial Revolution were on the horizon in 1787, and the stirrings of democratic government were beginning to be felt even in Europe.

Could the Founders have envisioned such things as Social Security or the G.I. Bill; probably the two most successful pieces of social legislation ever devised? Could they have envisioned the CCC and WPA of the 1930's, the Manhattan

Project, the Marshall Plan, the REA, the Interstate Highway System, the Space Program, Landing on the Moon?

Would they have approved of these landmark achievements of government? We'll never know the answer to that question, of course. We do know, however, that they trusted the collective will of the people working through their elected representatives.

Capitalism and Free-markets work! They act to produce new wealth of goods and services in abundant quantities. The Concepts proposed in this book are of the highest compliment to a capitalist free-market economic system, and to the wisdom of our Founders in providing flexibility in our Constitution.

The prosperous nations of the world, those nations that have led the way in developing the technology and increasing the store of knowledge that has enabled not only their own people, but those of other countries, to lessen drudgery and live better and longer lives, have done so under governments that preserve capitalism and meddle only to regulate as needed, and to promote the very modest sharing of both inherent and created wealth that actually works to increase the creation of new wealth for everyone.

◆   ◆   ◆

The promise of our Nation, and of this book, began on June 15, 1215, on the Meadow at Runnymede, beside the Thames, where King John, to avoid a civil war, signed a 'Great Charter' which came to be better known later as the Magna Carta.

It was here that the vague idea of self-government of the people and by the people, as opposed to the absolute power of kings, emperors or petty tyrants was born. 5-1/2 centuries of evolution, definition and refinement of this radical idea led to the revolt of English colonists on the east coast of the American continent against the taxation and subordination imposed, without representation, by the King of England. After a long and exhausting, but victorious, War for Independence, the English colonies became free to chart their own destiny. By 1787, they were ready to gather together to form a Federal union. They convened in May of that year and adjourned after signing the Constitution of the United States of America on September 17th, 1787

◆   ◆   ◆

In the political discourse and noise of our Nation, the emblematic virtues of the Constitution, particularly the Bill of Rights, are generally agreed on by Republicans, Democrats, Conservatives, Liberals, Libertarians, the Right and the Left. Issues of how much freedom of personal behavior we ought to allow ourselves (Guns, Drugs, Prostitution, Gambling, Abortion, etc.) somewhat predictably, and tediously, divide into Left and Right. On great National issues (War, Foreign Trade, Foreign Involvement, Aid to Foreign and Domestic Disaster Victims, Bailouts, the Environment, the place of Religion)) there is considerable crossing back-and-forth over party and ideological lines.

But, the real internecine struggle in our country is over the distribution of both the inherent and the created wealth of the Nation. The Right believes that, inherently, all wealth ought to belong to the individual who earned it or otherwise acquired it. The Right resists all taxation that is intended to distribute any small portion of 'their' money to others for whatever reason. (Well—, not quite; the Right often favors bailouts of corporations and other nations under the rubric of 'preserving economic stability'.) The Right views all measures that smell of adjustment of the distribution of wealth as an infringement on their personal freedom. The Left, on the other hand, is constantly pressing for ways, some devious, some open, to transfer wealth from the richer to the poorer.

But there's a previous side to the present story. From the earliest days of the Industrial Revolution and the beginnings of interchangeable parts and the mass production of product, the actual menial labor of production became less-and-less important compared to the value of organization and the accumulation of capital that enabled the further acceleration of production. As labor began to see the growing disparity between their incomes and the incomes of the managers and owners, they became increasingly restless and demanding of redress. But, because government, then as now, was more compliant to the needs and wishes of the accumulators of wealth, labor's early attempts to organize were resisted and thwarted by laws and actions designed to enhance the power of capital.

Fueling the growing disparity of incomes that more-and-more favored the rich in an industrial society was the axiomatic reality that small advantages of talent, brains and luck resulted in not proportional but *wide* advantages in the acquisition of wealth and power. The net effect was that for 100-plus years of industrialization, until about 1933, there was a de facto and distorted 'redistribution of created wealth' from labor to capital. Compounding this distortion of the benefit from industrialization was the obvious reality that increased wealth enabled its possessors to actually obtain title to a larger share of the natural resources that were the birthright equally of every American.

It comes down to this: You, the readers of this book, and we, the authors, are, almost by definition, in the upper half of the population in capabilities, creativity and energy. We will prosper more because of the 'edge' we've got. But, perhaps we'd feel better and maybe live easier, if we could make life a little better and a little less stressful for those folks, our countrymen and our neighbors, who work hard to clean the hotel rooms, who fix the streets, who repair the utility lines, and, bottom line, who attend to our safety, comfort and convenience in a myriad of boring and tedious jobs?

◆   ◆   ◆

At one point during the writing of this book, I asked Lois, a flaming liberal, why she was so deadset against Conservatives and Conservatism. Her quick response:

"I don't see why we can't have a country where people can make all the millions they want, and we can still, as a National responsibility, help people scrunched at or near the bottom, for whatever reason, to have a little better life. If we can't do both these things, what have we accomplished as a Nation?"

Lois' response was a nice warm-and-fuzzy liberal one. Problem is: Most people, the man (and woman) in the street, mostly clean, conservative by nature, and hard-working, don't think much about the folks at the bottom. They figure it's simple justice; the working poor got there by their own bad judgment (dropped out of school, too many kids too soon, drank too much) or by their just plain laziness. Conservatives especially don't want their hard-earned dollars siphoned off in taxes to support 'them'. ("Let 'em go down to the nearest Red Cross, or United Way, or Salvation Army and beg if they need help"). Who the Conservative mindset really favors are the entrepreneurs, the managers, the organizers, the risk-takers, the top brass and the well-off. Conservatives have never met a money-making corporate executive they didn't like. And, of course, the Conservative mind is contradicted on the subject of abortion; they call it 'murder', but they don't have the stomach to call for the jailing of the mother.

To the Conservative mind, 'labor', the guys and gals who put the nut on the bolt, or pick the strawberries, or drive the trucks are peasants; they don't deserve any more pay than the guy who's got the 'gold' decides to pay them. To a Conservative, Minimum Wage Laws are a bad idea; they work against the poor by creating unemployment. (Although it's a charge that's never been proven.)

No matter how you slice it, when you start talking about a little bit of leveling by any adjustment of the distribution of income (or wealth) through the heavy hand of taxation, you're talking 'red meat' for Conservatives and Libertarians. They hurl 'Socialist' or 'Communist' around with careless ease. They figure they earned every dollar they got 'all by themselves', and that, by god, they ought to get to keep it all. What drives 'em up the wall about Liberals (read Democrats) is that 'those guys' are always trying to figure out ways to take money from the person who earned it and give it to somebody who didn't. (Any of that, of course, to a Conservative is Socialism or Communism.)

Liberals, and the Left in general, have several serious problems, too. Most Liberals are completely fuzzy-headed about the courage and dedication it takes to produce new wealth. And there's no question that some of the most light-headed and idiotic people, including some politicians and celebrities, make off-the-cuff counter-cultural remarks that disgrace the cause of true Liberalism.

True Liberals have the idea that nobody in these United States gets rich all by themselves; they feel that all the rest of us nameless and faceless ones pitch in every day to build, maintain and protect the system and the infrastructure the rich use on their way to getting rich. Liberals have another idea; they believe that it's in everybody's best economic interest, both rich and poor, for the entire Nation to be well-fed, well-clothed and well-housed.

And to the Liberal's shame, they have never made a solid case for proving that the killing of an unborn child is <u>not</u> murder. That case is made for Judeo-Christian believers in Genesis 2:7 where it clearly states that God created human life only by first '—forming man from the dust of the ground—', then '—by breathing into his nostrils the breath of life—'; a clear metaphor for concluding that human life does <u>not</u> begin until the first breath is drawn after birth.

Liberals dislike the Right so much for the Right's *perceived* selfishness and indifference to the value of the tedious and hard work of the laborer, that they don't even listen when the Right does makes good sense on a lot of issues. Liberals are so ignorant of the virtues of Capitalism that it's hard for them to make sensible suggestions to improve it. A continuing problem endured by the Liberal-Left is that they have no leaders who speak sanely, logically and forcefully, and with good common sense. People on the Left have a hard time giving any credit to, or even defending, the Capitalist Free-market type of economy that has produced the abundance of wealth they're so anxious to redistribute. And the Liberal-Left generally, and casually, dismisses that passion of the Right—religion, especially the Christian religion—as irrelevant.

Finally, Liberalism faces a quandary, a 'body-count drain' of sorts. Policies set in place during the 1930's to stimulate economic growth and to provide a modicum of redistribution of income and a small degree of 'social security' have worked so well that millions of people have become so wealthy that they hate taxes and 'social programs' and become conservatives and libertarians.

◆   ◆   ◆

Now you have an idea why we struggled so hard and argued so much in writing this book!

On the one hand, we both have a deep respect and admiration for our Constitution. We find it incredible that at that singular moment in time, in Philadelphia in that hot summer of 1787, a group of men (yes, all white and some of them slave owners) from various walks of life, some highly educated—some not, came together; and from that blending of intellects, experiences and instincts they produced a Document that not only has endured for 215 years but probably has been responsible, more than any other single factor, for our becoming the richest, strongest and most moral Nation the world has ever seen. We have a strong dedication to the concept of personal freedom that's at the heart and soul of that Constitution.

On the other hand, we both have a passion to suggest new ways of governing our Nation that will enhance personal opportunity and make life better for everyone, including those among us who are not the 'best and the brightest'. And this passion of ours extends to a simultaneous goal of substantially reducing the size, cost, influence and intrusiveness of the Federal Government while, at the same time, bringing more stability and growth to our economy. Yes; our Nation can simultaneously accomplish all of these things.

What is our Nation? (Here's where the rubber meets the road.) Is it simply a place with borders where we establish military and legal systems, and a monetary environment, to guarantee that '—the race goes to the swiftest, and the devil take the hindmost—'; or is it the home of a kind of 'extended family' that willingly taxes itself in part to insure that the lesser among us have at least a minimal education, basic health care and an otherwise decent chance at a good life?

It's quite possible that all domestic politics is summed up in the question posed by the preceding paragraph.

Our Constitution, brilliant in its formulation, was drafted in a time when the Nation was largely agrarian, thinly settled, and occupied only a slice of land along the eastern seaboard. Because we have grown into a complex industrial and post-industrial Nation of 280 million people, with many teeming megalopolises, and thousands of smaller cities and towns, with open spaces of forests and waters and broad fields of agriculture, standing ocean-to-ocean across an entire continent, we have found it necessary to add 16 amendments beyond the first 10 (the Bill of Rights) to adapt the Constitution to our changing needs.

We've invented and we've risked, we've planned and we've organized, we've dug and we've built, we've fought and we've died. For 215 years we've used the brains and the brawn of native and immigrant, and we're now the most productive Nation on the planet. And on at least 10 occasions during those 215 years, averaging once every generation, we have asked our young people, the sons and daughters of the working people, to risk their lives on domestic and foreign battlefields to guarantee the safety and freedom of the rest of us. As we write this, we're about to ask them again.

Opportunity for the individual for a good life and for personal improvement in this Nation is now greater than it has ever been, and is greater than in any other Nation. We have ended official discrimination toward races and toward women. We have established a degree of a social safety net for those who suffer misfortune. But we also have urban blight, we have poverty, we have a large drug culture and we keep discovering 'new' diseases in our midst. We have wasted effort in government, and a bloated and inefficient health care system. We endure cruel and unusual punishment from our awkward tax system and in the distribution of subsidies and 'favors' from our Federal Government. Each year we go through the expensive charade of taxing extra money from the residents and businesses of every State, then giving that money back to the same States. Why?

Our Constitution is silent[2] on using the regulatory power of Government, and, yes, the tax system, to try to smooth the wrinkles in our social fabric; or is it silent[2]? We're fully aware that Capitalism and the Free-market insures the highest output of goods and services at the lowest cost, and that Article 1, Section 8 of the Constitution prescribes only certain specific functions and duties of the Federal Government; to wit, the national defense, a system of justice, coining money, punishing counterfeiters and pirates, issuing and protecting patents, establishing laws on naturalization and bankruptcies, regulating interstate commerce and borrowing money on the credit of the United States..

Everything considered, do you really believe the Founders intended to prohibit the Federal Government, acting legislatively, and through the tax system, 215 years later, from engaging in any activity that was not specifically enumerated or foreseen in the year 1787?

Concluding:

There's nothing inherently wrong with Free-market Capitalism—

• There's nothing wrong with people being able to make, ethically, all the money they can—

---

2.   On the 'silence' of the Constitution, let's talk about that, not in legalese, or Supreme Court terminology, but in good ol' American common sense; and try to see what the Founders meant, and what they might say if they came back now. (Right here is where we drive the Libertarians and the hard-line Conservatives up the wall.) In the Preamble, and again in Article 1,Section 8, the Founders saw fit to include the phraseology '—promote (and provide for) the General Welfare. Therefore, aren't we entitled to at least ask whether they (the Founders) would be shocked If they saw that 215 years later the Federal Government (still a representative body of the People according to their original architecture) decided to use the power to tax to assure that a portion of the bounty we all now contribute to producing and protecting be used to enhance the overall economy and the security and health of all the citizens that comprise this complex Nation. They might, of course, even refer us to their own 10th Amendment to the Constitution that "—reserves to the States—or to the People those powers not (specifically)—delegated to the United States—'"

- There's nothing wrong with the personal freedom to behave as you see fit so long as you do not harm others—

- There's nothing wrong with privately-practiced religion if you choose to believe in a 'higher being'. (There is, of course, a cause for worry and watchfulness if a high public official, constructing public policy, is intensely religious and believes in the occult, in mythology or in the supernatural.)—

We do have all of these freedoms in this great Nation; but maybe, just maybe, a nation, especially a great Nation like ours, needs the glue of some small bit of sharing of our overall good fortune among all of our citizens. Maybe each citizen 'owns' one share of stock in our country, and we ought periodically to declare a dividend.

The REPUBLICAN PARADOX

The paradox of the *new* Republican Party—

The preponderance of the white middle class, the upper-middle class, business owners, the executive class, the new rich and much of the Hispanic population are viscerally stirred by the 'conservative' message of patriotism, self-reliance, the work ethic, traditional moral standards, belligerence, tough-on-crime, family values, lower taxes, religion and the wholesale ridicule and vilification of 'liberals'. They vote Republican because they 'hate give-away programs'. They're firm in their philosophy that government ought not do anything for people that people can do for themselves; a virtuous affirmation of the dignity and power of the individual, but a denial of the multiplying effect of community.

But, most of these same people don't realize that the *new* Republican philosophy, the barely-hidden agenda of the ambitious new young party leaders who cotton to the religious right, calls for rolling back the social and economic programs instituted since 1932; a rollback that would have devastating effects on their lifestyle and would dramatically change the whole character of the Nation they grew up in. These young leaders weren't yet born when the men who came of age during the Great Depression made their comfortable life possible by wading through the hells of Normandy, Iwo Jima and Okinawa, and by freezing their cojones off at Bastogne. They were pre-schoolers when Brown v. Board. Of Education ignited the successful Civil Rights revolution. They were hardly teen-agers when the Pill and 'The Feminine Mystique' changed life forever.

These prosperous new 'Republicans' simply don't 'get it'; they don't 'get' the idea that their very prosperity and their good life style have grown out of the soil that was made fertile by the liberal policies laid down by the older and much wiser leaders of both parties in the 1930's and on through the 1960's. It was these leaders who saved Free-market Capitalism and restored its vitality by protecting it from its own destructive excesses.

Because capitalism has been allowed to work its magic in an orderly way, we have created widespread prosperity, a cleaner and more healthful environment, more personal opportunity, hundreds of new millionaires and a score of billionaires. And, during this same 35-40 year period, our nation expanded personal freedom by codifying into law the equal rights of women and minorities. (In the interest of full disclosure, however, it has to be said that many of the older 'good' Republicans had to be dragged kicking and screaming into the world of 'equal rights'; i.e., the 20th Century honoring of the 13th and 14th Amendments to the Constitution.)

What's so bad about success?

Make no mistake; 'rollback' to the 'glory days' of laissez-faire and low taxes is the intention of the Tom DeLay's, the Trent Lott's, the James Inhofe's and the George W. Bush's, the present group of leaders of the Republican Party, and of the Christian Coalition. These people are relentless; and their co-ordinated handmaidens are the present group of sarcastic, vitriolic, pompous and unctuous talkshow hosts and authors like Rush Limbaugh, Dennis Prager, Sean Hannity, Larry Elder, 'The Savage Nation', Michael Medved and Ann Coulter.

All of the above engage in their destructive tasks praising God and asking him to uniquely bless America and turn us into a theo-democracy while wearing red, white and blue banners calling for restoring morality, decency and war-making to the republic. These people, by their actions and their statements, believe in the Christian Coalition's stated position that "There's no way for America to be good if she's not godly (sic)", and that disallowing prayer in schools "is a deception from Satan (sic)." (Quotes are from a CNN 2002 Election Report dated October 11, 2002, carried on the CNN website.)

Adherents to Republicanism, Conservatism, Libertarianism (or whatever you call it) don't realize that a nation without Social Security (or a guaranteed equivalent), without Medicare, without a minimum wage, without a Fair Labor Standards Act, without strong environmental standards, without strong civil rights legislation, without publicly-owned National Parks and National Monuments, without universal public education, without a federally-stabilized banking system, without aggressive soil erosion programs, without an Interstate Highway System and with no SEC, FAA, FDA, FHA, FCC, FDIC, REA, NIH, OSHA, Hoover, Bonneville, or Grand Coulee dams or TVA, and without a high 'wall of separation' between church and state, would be a far less pleasant and rewarding nation in which to live and raise a family.

One need only look at nations which have illiberal, weak or theocratic governments to see the want, misery, disease and dehumanization such governments bring on their people. Tour through much of our own Latin America, or the Caribbean areas, or through the Middle East or Africa, or through many of the smaller countries of Asia; most Americans would be appalled at seeing the conditions in which most of the people of the world live. Women, particularly, would be shocked to see the way their gender is relegated to second-class status or worse

Have all the programs, these Federal Acts, Bureaus and initiatives cost tax dollars? Of course! It's called 'civilization'.

Wouldn't it cost all of us far less to simply have a government that adhered strictly to the Constitution and had no programs designed to enhance life for everyone? Of course it would!

Wouldn't it cost all of us far less to have a government that cared not about the welfare of the lesser talented, the lesser capable, the less lucky, and the lower paid among us, but simply stayed out of the game and let the race go to the swiftest and send the losers down to the nearest charity and beg? Of course it would!

Isn't there a severe the tax bite on the middle—and upper-middle classes to support all the government expenditures made to stabilize and secure both the producers and the consumers in our economy? Of course there is.

Has there been waste? Naturally!

But all equations have two sides; let's ask ourselves a few questions:

- Isn't it probable that all incomes before taxes are higher than they would otherwise be if there were no 'government' to provide stability and security for the conduct of business, and to see that there's a small amount of adjustment of income and wealth to alleviate poverty, to educate the young and to assure a broad spread of purchasing power.

  - Would we really like to live in a libertarian country where there was limited stability and security and no attempt made to assure wide distribution of purchasing power?

  - Do we know anyone, or know of anyone, who has been prevented by high taxes from becoming wealthy?

Obviously, there's a balance to be struck. Totalitarian-type government and massive leveling is ridiculous; it's been tried in many countries with uniformly disastrous results. Shared poverty and a filthy environment is not something for any nation to aspire to.

Now, we come to the other Party, the Democrats—

Where are the Democrats who really fight the battles of true liberalism? We can't find them anywhere. Too often, when we do hear of Democrats, it's because they're involved in some moral scandal; Jim Wright, Bill Clinton, Tom Harkin, Paul Patton, Robert Torricelli.

Where are the Democrats who ought to be pounding the podium and demanding a clear and unambiguous look at evil in the world, and demanding as well a comprehensive Universal Health Care program, an end to the vicious, counter-productive, invasive and wasteful Income Tax and FICA, an end to all of the bureaucratically-wasteful Subsidies and selective Entitlements, a new look at the murderously destructive Drug War, and a powerful Manhattan Project-type of clean energy research program?

Where are the Democrats who can articulate and defend in a powerful way a vision of where this country ought to go in the next ten years? The only Democrats we see are those who argue mildly against Republican retrogression, or who advocate baby steps and hunkering down?

Why have the Democrats allowed the crazies among them to go unchallenged. We're talking about the crazies who advocate moral relativism, or who tend to overlook evil, or who defend socialism and devalue free-market capitalism, or who consistently engage in anti-American rhetoric to get attention.

The rabid and vulgar rants of the right-wing talk show hosts are only slightly more odious than the complete lack of vision and new ideas on the part of the Bill Clinton's, the Tom Daschle's, the Dick Gephardt's and the Phil Donahue's.

Where in the present leadership of the Democratic party are the FDR's, the Harry Truman's, the John Kennedy's, the Lyndon Johnson's? Where's the vision? Who's articulating any 21st Century equivalents of the Marshall Plan, the G.I. Bill, REA, Interstate Highways, the Space Program or Landing on the Moon? Is there nothing left to do? Is there nothing that can inspire us to be better than we are? Are the Daschle's, the Gephardt's and the McAuliffe's the best we can do?

Are there any Democrats who really understand what their basic political philosophy is? Do they understand what liberalism means? Liberalism is a proud tradition of declaring the worth and dignity of every person, and of using the concept of community responsibility to enhance everyone's life. Why have we allowed the opposition to so co-opt the also important concepts of patriotism and moral values that the word 'liberal' has become an object of ridicule and derision?

It's really no mystery that the 'little people' are leaving the two major political parties in droves, and refusing to contribute. They're leaving because they realize that the Republicans and the Democrats are morphing into a single force totally in the control of the fat cats of all stripes. Time-after-time the folks who are trying to bring some new ideas into the democratic process through the medium of a third party are frozen out of the debates or even physically restrained from entering the venue where a debate is going on. (The latter happened recently in Los Angeles where the Green Party candidate was prevented from entering a hall where a debate between the Republican and the Democratic candidates for Governor of California was being held.)

◆   ◆   ◆

Fortunately, our Founders did such a great job that with all of the hiccups and all of the corruption, with all of the vacuousness and with all of the blows to our sensibilities, the Republic will endure. We're a great Nation, and the final truth is that the great decisions of our Nation grow out of the common-sense driven consensus of the folks who spurn party-line allegiance, but who know in their hearts what's best for America.

AS A GREAT NATION, WE CAN DO BETTER!

Conservatism, Liberalism, Libertarianism—Government and the People

Our views of Conservatism in this chapter were formed as an amalgam from observations of people with conservative leanings in private conversation, from participating in numerous formal discussion groups, and from listening to notably conservative public figures in both political and religious venues across the Nation.

Surprisingly, it has taken us long lifetimes of political observation and writing to realize that 'Conservative thinking' by the average person is a strong belief in his own mental and moral strength and toughness, in his own ruggedness and self-reliance, in his own integrity, in his own capabilities, his patriotism, and in his full entitlement to every dollar he earns. His corollary belief is that everyone ought to have these same qualities and ought to be sufficiently disciplined to live within certain vaguely-prescribed 'norms' of attitude and behavior, and within the income they can earn on their own. These beliefs direct the Conservative to oppose any measures that address income disparities; measures such as the Minimum Wage, or Welfare or National Health Care To now understand the individualistic (and 'strength') mindset of the Conservative is to explain:

—the wide appeal of raucous, tough-talking and polemical 'talk radio' shows[3],
—the belligerence of the Conservative and his attraction to the military side of national defense, military superiority of the United States and pre-emptive military action.

—the support of strict interpretation of the Constitution (a distinctly 'conservative' document).
—the awe of, and deference to, individual and corporate wealth and power,

Conservatives (and Libertarians) tend to resist most environmental protections and most measures designed to protect the public from unnecessary hazards as invasions of private property rights and costly to the economy. Conservatives (and Libertarians) believe that market alternatives such as zealous protection of property rights and the use of insurance will be sufficient to protect the environment and to insure the necessary safety measures in the workplace and in consumer products. However, Conservatives (and many Libertarians) may have some rethinking to do:

Modern 'Liberalism' began with FDR in 1933. During the 70-odd years since then is when the trend toward bigger government and more regulation of business gained new momentum and effect.

Since the beginning of that increased trend, we saved and secured our banking system, we emerged from the Great Depression, fought and won World War II (where we tripled our industrial output), rebuilt war-ravaged economies through the Marshall Plan, educated our veterans through the G.I. Bill, wired up and telephone-serviced every farm in the Nation through the REA, saved millions of acres of farm land from erosion through government programs of Soil Conservation, built the Interstate Highway System, commercialized jet aircraft travel, launched the Civil Rights movement, conquered Polio, launched NASA, landed a Man on the Moon and explored the fringes of the Solar System, cleaned up our Environment, doubled gasoline mileage for our cars, fought two more major wars, (Korea and Vietnam) won the Cold War by staring down and outspending our powerful enemy, the Soviet Unjon, _and_ increased our standard of living across-the-board.

We created some of the world's largest corporations, an unbelievable number of new millionaires, and more than a score of billionaires, while essentially ending poverty among our Seniors. We are starting more new businesses and more of our

---

3.   Another word needs to be said about most Conservative talk show hosts:
      There is little in their ranting that addresses the kinder, gentler side of human nature. Perhaps it's because they all believe, as Dennis Prager has often said, that we are all evil by nature; that each of us must constantly struggle against the dark side of our nature. Do you believe that?

young people are in college today than ever before. We have enjoyed an explosion of new technology and an unimaginable increase in the speed and variety of communications and in the array of products and services that make life more comfortable and safer.

We have incubated a geometric expansion of knowledge in the sciences and in medicine. We have added untold acres of parkland, greenbelts and playgrounds.

We have expanded both the consciousness and the reality of personal freedoms and rights, and we have ended official racial and gender discrimination. We have become the most Christian and patriotic nation in the world. We have welcomed and given succor and opportunity to millions of immigrants who came to our Nation to build a better life.

And with all of that, our Nation stands today at the apex of our power, wealth and influence in the world. Now, the curmudgeons among us, confronted with these facts, may grumble, "—ya' but think what it might have been if—". But anything other than the historical evidence is pure speculation or conjecture..

Because Conservatives believe in a sharp line of demarcation between 'good' and 'evil', they tend toward harsh and unremitting punishment of offending individuals or nations.

Understanding the Conservative mindset also explains the disdain for Liberalism by many Conservatives. Modern Liberalism has become the voice of the weak, the less capable, the less lucky, the less disciplined, the under-represented, the poor, the lazy, the minorities. Modern Liberalism is always the voice calling for moderation, for negotiation, for permissiveness, for mercy, for help from government, for complicated solutions, for a search for mitigating circumstances, for a tolerant view of evil. None of these 'causes' stirs the blood or the viscera; nor do they have much currency in the 'Conservative' mind.

Modern 'Liberalism' confounds the 'rugged individualist' who bristles at 'communitarianism' (he calls it 'Socialism'), and who resents someone 'getting something for nothing'. Modern Liberalism is not a message to stir one's basic human passions. It's a search for equality, it's a message of toleration of differences and foibles, of protection of the environment and of public health and safety (all of which Liberals view as beneficial, rather than detrimental, to the economy), and of leveling of extremes. Frankly, the Liberal economic message is a message of some 'redistribution of income', that super-anathema of Conservatives. (And, in fairness to Conservative belief, any justification for redistribution of income in the Constitution hangs on the thin thread of the two references to '—the general welfare—'; in the Preamble and in Article 1, Section 8)

Summing up: In our United States in this year 2003, Conservatives and Liberals agree that the capitalist free-market system is the best means of producing wealth and allowing individuals to benefit richly from their success. Their political differences trace back to how some of that wealth is reckoned and distributed, and to their feelings about the importance of religion. Obviously, there are individual exceptions to the generalizations that follow, but in the main Conservatism is a soul-stirring message of strength, sturdiness, self-reliance, the-race-goes—to-the-swiftest, 'this-is-what-built-America', the-money-I-earn-is-all-mine, take-care-of-your-own, behave-yourself, live-by-the-rules-of-God-and-the-Constitution. Conservatives tend to distrust majority rule; prefer a republican (representative) form of governing.

Liberalism is a soft-edged un-exciting message of share-some-of-the-wealth, don't-be-too-judgmental, let's-use-government-to-ease-burdens, not-too-sure-about-God's-place-in-our-life, not-too-sure-that-the-Constitution-forbids-using-government-to-do-good-things. Liberals tend to trust majority rule;prefer a more directly democratic form of governing.

There's an irony here: There's a strong affinity between those who are Christian fundamentalist believers and those who are hard-line political Conservatives. Strange; because there's a strong convergence between the charitable, humble, peace-loving, accommodating and forgiving philosophy of Jesus Christ himself, and the philosophies of modern Liberalism. It seems apparent that if the Christ we know from the Bible were alive today, he would be a Liberal And there's another irony present in this book: Knowing full well how Conservatives feel about any 'redistribution of income', We're determined that in the following pages we're going to convince them of the wisdom of two changes in the socio-economic structure of our Nation that clearly are based on that conservative bugaboo. (And we can only hope that the sunburst of logic and appeal of the other change—ending all Federal taxes—will illuminate their vision in considering those above-mentioned two changes as enhancing the security and prosperity of our Nation and of the citizens who go to work every day to make this country happen.)

Hard-line Conservatives face a challenge of reality. Since 1932, our Nation has been governed under a generally leftist philosophy of major interventions by the Federal government to level social and economic disparities and promote financial security and higher incomes for lower level working people. Since 1932 the Federal Government has also initiated huge economic projects designed to contribute to the overall wealth of the nation; projects beyond the capabilities and interest of private capital; e.g., REA, FHA, TVA, Bonneville, Grand Coulee and numerous other dams, Soil Conservation, the Marshall Plan, the G.I. Bill, the Space Program, and the Interstate Highway Program. These Federal actions, these manifestations of leftist philosophy, went far beyond the 'enumerated powers' specified in Article 1, Section 8 of the Constitution.

More individual prosperity—
A longer average life span—
Better health—
More National wealth—
More emphasis on the personal rights covered by the First Ten Amendments—
A cleaner environment—
More open space preservation—
More park land—
Less drudge and dangerous labor—
More racial and gender justice—
More public consciousness and discussion of moral issues—
The highest level of international prestige and influence—
A higher level of religious consciousness—
More leisure time—
More home ownership—
More economic opportunity for young people—
More security for the aged—
Less poverty—
Greater agricultural production with less soil erosion—
Higher levels of education—
Technological superiority—
Safer automobiles—
Safer airlines
Better and safer roads—
Safer consumer products—
Safer pharmaceuticals—

Safer workplace environments—
Regulated stock markets for safer investment—
Regulated and safe nuclear energy—
Organized natural disaster relief—

When confronted with the above listing, the only response of the 'right' can be the teeth-grinding and speculative, "Ya', but *we* could have done better."

Conservatives, of course, get the opportunity every two years through the election process to take over the direction of the country. 'Conservatism' is a thoroughly legitimate message; but part of the problem faced by Conservatives in getting their message across is that they're ill-served by their spokesmen on 'talk radio'. I'm talking here about the likes of the religion-oriented and pompously moralizing Dennis Prager, the ranting, negative and paranoiac Rush Limbaugh, the pedantic and shrill Sean Hannity, the copy-cat conservative Mike Gallagher, and the unctuous Michael Medved.

But to the credit of the Conservative side are the contentious but often reasonable Bill O'Reilly, the thoughtful George Will, the erudite William Buckley, the challenging Bob Novak, the young and articulate Tucker Carlson, and, of course, that grand old father of libertarian conservatism, Milton Friedman.

Liberals have their share of burdens to carry, too: The charming but ineffective and ideologically-impotent Bill Clinton, the mushy and boring Larry King, the untrustworthy Jesse Jackson, the garrulous and one-track minded Clinton-defender James Carville, and the voiceless' Dick Gephardt and Tom Daschle.

It would be good for our American democracy, which thrives on and improves itself by vigorous debate, if there were even a few articulate and persuasive spokesmen who could carry the philosophical case for modern Liberalism. Radio's Michael Jackson and Jim Hightower and television's Phil Donahue are good at expressing themselves, and they support generally-liberal positions; but they are never out-front advocates and definers of liberal philosophy. There's a real question whether any of today's politicians or talking heads who speak for the Democratic Party have a clue as to what the guiding philosophy of the party is.

WHERE ARE THE GIANTS?

We descendants of European and Latin cultures, with a lot of help from the descendants of Africans, who, to our shame, we subjected to slavery long after the rest of the civilized world abolished it, have built a prosperous and healthy Nation; and, in the 20th century, we were instrumental in ending the scourges of Communism, Fascism, Nazism and old-fashioned Imperialism. But I get the feeling that prosperity has tired us and made us indifferent to the plights of those among us who suffer unnecessary hardship and anxiety. Yes, when a real and easily definable disaster occurs—an earthquake in California, a flood on the Mississippi, a drought in the South, the destruction of two buildings in New York—we dig into our jeans and send money to the victims, and the Federal Government sends additional millions of our tax dollars. But what about the thousands of ongoing personal misfortunes that strike every day? Could there be some way to mitigate the consequences of unforeseeable and uninvited individual disasters? Or is that beyond the scope of any advanced society? Perhaps that's a subject for another book.

At this point in our discussion of ideas, we need to touch on the concept of 'community'. We have a great many friends of Conservative and Libertarian persuasion who recoil at any concept of 'community' that indicates a body politic responsibility toward individual distress, or at *anything* in the economic arena outside of the specific purposes stated in the Constitution, or at anything that smacks of coercion or of redistribution of income through the tax system. They believe that there ought be no 'public assistance' or welfare programs. In the Libertarian world, individual cases of hardship or need would be handled by churches, charity or individual benevolence. Also in the Libertarian world, there would be no laws or regulations governing corporate behavior, except in cases of force or fraud; and no Anti-trust Laws, no Minimum Wage Law, no Worker Safety Laws, no Pension Protection Laws, no Collective Bargaining Laws, no FAA, no FDA, no SEC, no NIH, no OSHA, no EPA.

Libertarians believe that any person has the right to do with his life whatever he sees fit so long as he does not harm another by force or fraud; To Libertarians, taxes for any purpose other than those explicitly authorized in the Constitution (National Defense, a System of Justice, etc.) are literally 'theft' because they represent the taking of money by government fiat (tyranny of the majority) from one individual in order to give it to another individual, or to build public facilities. In other words, Libertarians are haunted and horrified by the specter of 'redistribution of income' through the 'coercion' of the tax system. Libertarians, you see, disagree with the concept of Public Education, Public Libraries, Public Roads, Public Lands, National Parks, etc. in the sense that any of those functions would be owned by government and supported by taxes. In the Libertarian view, Education ought to be an individual responsibility, and roads ought to be 'toll' roads. Public Lands and National Parks ought to be sold to private interests, and Environmental Protection and Clean-up would be handled through the market and judicial systems.

We've dwelled on the Libertarian philosophy because its emphasis on personal freedom and the verity of the Constitution is compelling; the major parties, Republicans and Democrats, have much to learn from them. We agree with the Libertarians on maximizing personal freedom by such things as ending the Drug War, and by using a Voucher System as part of Public Education; and we agree with them that the Capitalist System and Free Markets are unexcelled as the best and the most proven way of producing wealth. But doesn't *Real* Conservatism depart sharply from the negative Libertarian concept of 'community'? Doesn't Real Conservatism hold that the —'General Welfare'—statements in the Preamble and in Section 8 of Article 1 of the Constitution are sufficient authorization to use the influence of government to blunt the excesses and distortions of the market system and to assure minimum standards of living and decency for all citizens, even though some of the measures may require some minor 'redistribution of income'?

We believe we came together 215 years ago as a democratic republic to do more than merely protect ourselves from foreign invaders and provide a safe environment for healthy, strong and industrious individuals to grow and flower; though those are indeed worthy goals. We believe we also came together to use the power of 'community' and nationhood insure that the lesser among us have some shelter from the harshness of unrestrained competition or greedy monopoly and are given a 'leg up' to help them achieve some degree of security in their lives. What benefits them, benefits us all through a more secure and happier society.

All of us dislike paying taxes, but for both Libertarians and Conservatives, a short, very short, roll-call of some of the benefits that the Federal Government, both through direct action, and through legislation, has brought to our lives is in order:

Assistance to the States in providing a basic education for every child………

Vaccination programs for children……….

Cleaner water and cleaner air……...

A more prosperous older generation; less burden on their children........

NIH health research and The Center for Disease Control.........

Stock fraud protection through the SEC.........

Safer work places........

An Interstate Highway System.........

Power and Irrigation from Federally-constructed dams........

Electricity and Telephone service to all rural areas.........

Space exploration...........

Doubled the average gas mileage of our cars.............

Seat belts, air bags, more crash-resistant cars...........

A stable banking system.........

An efficient Coast Guard for safer boating........

Preservation of important land, landmarks, monuments, and parks through the Department of the Interior.........

Nutrition labels on all foods to help us stay healthy........

Hardliners can say that all of those things that have added to our lives could have and would have been accomplished through the operation of free markets. That's speculation; the simple fact is, they *were* done through the actions of the Federal Government even though none of them was within the enumerated powers of Article 1, Section 8 of the Constitution.

Another word has to be said here about 'taxes'. Yes, we do pay somewhere between 35 and 50 percent of our income in taxes (combined Federal, State, Local) to the various levels of government. But don't we all need to ask ourselves whether we might, in fact, only be making the high incomes we do because government provides, protects and insures the business and legal environment that enables us to earn those incomes. Would our incomes be what they are if our Nation weren't secure in its borders and coastlines, if we didn't have a stable banking system, a stable currency, a stable and predictable legal system, a secure and regulated investment structure, police protection, fire protection, a thoroughly-pervasive educational system, a well-developed transportation system (including the Interstate Highway System), a well-developed communications system, and an assured and low-cost food supply.

In one way or another, the sometimes bungling and costly, but sometimes efficient, governments at all levels have had a hand in creating the peaceful and orderly milieu, the 'quality of life', that enable businesses and individuals to prosper.

A QUESTION—

> Did we of the World War II generation do something wrong? It is our sons and daughters who now have the political helm of our ship of state, but none of them in either of the major parties has exhibited the courage to risk their comfortable and trouble-free existence by getting out front with powerful table-pounding oratory demanding real change. They're smart, they're well-educated and they're technologically brilliant. But where is the vision? Who will lay out a goal for what we'll achieve in the next ten years? Today we have the limited outlooks, the narrow visions, of the Bill Clinton's, the George W. Bush's, the Al Gore's, the Trent Lott's, the Richard Gephardt's, the Tom Daschle's and the Tom DeLay's. All they can think of is protecting what we have. My god!, we're better than that, aren't we?

WHERE ARE THE GIANTS?

Who do we have now who has the cojones to do the kinds of things that Harry Truman did; end the war in the Pacific with a bold decision to use the atomic bomb, desegregate the armed forces, initiate the G.I. Bill of Rights, support the Marshall Plan to rebuild Europe, introduce the first bill to provide National Health Care, and yes, even to fire a general who dared challenge his Commander-in Chief?

Who do we have now who would do, as Dwight Eisenhower did; preside over the wiring for electricity and telephone service of every farm in the Nation, appoint the Chief Justice whose court ended segregated schools and sounded the death knell of official discrimination in all areas of our life, and who, as Commander-in-Chief, punctuated that statement by sending troops to Little Rock to protect the kids starting to integrate the High School there, who initiated the Space Program, who began the Interstate Highway Program, and finally, in a departing act of courage and prescience, warned us against the danger of a too-powerful and ruthless 'military-industrial complex'?

Who do we have now who can command the turn of phrase and lay down the challenges of John Kennedy's "The torch has been passed to new generation", and "—ask not what your country can do for you; ask what you can do for your country." and "—within this decade we will land a man on the moon", and "Ich bin ein Berliner"? Or Ronald Reagan's "Shining city on a hill", or "—evil empire—", or "Mr. Gorbachev, tear down that wall!"? Or who do we have now who will force change at the pace of Lyndon Johnson who demanded and got the Civil Rights Act, the Voting Rights Act and Medicare, and began a War on Poverty?

Where are the new Martin Luther King's who will challenge us by saying things like, "—I have a dream—", and calls upon us "—to judge a person not by the color of their skin, but by the content of their character."?

Do we have in our midst a leader who can equal the boldness of Richard Nixon's initial trip to China; or who can renew out of the UN Charter, as Jimmy Carter did, a concept as bold and as clean as 'Human Rights'?

Where do we find a leader who will challenge us to let our 'reach exceed our grasp'? Who will lay on the table a challenging new idea to improve our Nation, and demand of the Congress, *"This we will do."*? Where can we find such people?

WHERE ARE THE GIANTS?

The 'vision' of our present crop of leaders consists of cutting taxes, erecting missile defenses, flailing away at pipsqueak terrorists, fighting off a recession, privatizing Social Security; in other words, 'hunkering down'. And, it puzzles us that we don't hear them decrying the enormous amount of wasted human effort going on around them in the government bureaucracies. In Bill Clinton's presidency, he appointed Al Gore to 're-invent' government. After 8 years of effort, we heard not one peep about deeply reforming, or eliminating, the most wasteful system of all—the Income Tax!

We hear 'leaders' of racial and ethnic groups shouting 'victimization'; We don't hear a word from them exhorting those minorities among us to become more than they think they can be.

Does all of this mean that we have become all that we can be? We don't want to believe that.

Does no one in charge see any way that we can take the next step to becoming an even better place to live and work and raise families? Is there no way we can use our present pre-eminent position in the family of Nations to find a bold stroke that can insure peace in the world for 100 years. Is 'finding and killing terrorists' all we're capable of? Don't we have some kind of ideas that go beyond that kind of timidity? We certainly did not cover ourselves with glory in Vietnam, or the Gulf War, or in Kosovo, or in Afghanistan.

And we say equally about our writers. Where are they? Where are the Harriet Beecher Stowe's, the Upton Sinclair's, the John Steinbeck's, the Milton Friedman's and, certainly, the Martin Luther King's, and the James Baldwin's, all of whose powerful writings were able to stir the complacencies of their times and lead to social and political change. Look around you in the library or bookstore where you're perusing *this* book; you won't find *one* other book that outlines definitive political ideas on what we can and must do to make America, and even the world, better for everyone. What you will find is brilliantly-written biographies or well-written histories of what used to be, or cheap peek-a-boo sensationalism about what 'is', or a deluge of inward-looking 'self-help' or 'moral guidance' books. Where are the books that try to tell us 'what our country *ought* to be, and can be'?

AS A GREAT NATION, WE CAN DO BETTER!

Socio-Political Ideas—Conservative vs. Liberal Viewpoints

To help you understand where we are with this book, we've tried, in the next few pages, to outline some of the fundamental philosophical differences between Conservatives and Liberals. These are, of course, broad generalizations. As witnessed by the increasing trend toward 'Independent' voting registration by both Republicans and Democrats, there is much crossover, shifting and convergence of political ideology among voters. More and more people are tending to evaluate issues on their perceived merit rather than on their party's 'official' position. The door for one, or even two new political parties is opening wider and wider. There's an increasing trend toward a broad interpretation of any 'restraints' on government actions in the Constitution; but also an increasing awareness of, and emphasis on, the 'rights' delineated in the first ten Amendments to the Constitution. We see both these trends as encouraging.

We've selected a number of important issues to try to draw distinctions between the two modes of political thought in America. It's striking to us that the 'Liberal' or 'Conservative' mindset is so deeply embedded in many people that their response to one or two key questions can predict what their response will be almost any issue raised from that point on. (Is it true as Benjamin Disraeli once observed: "Every little baby born alive, is either a little Lib-er-al or a little Con-ser-va-tyve."?

1. SECURITY—
Conservatives believe that 'security' in the national sense means only the physical defense of the Nation's territory, its people and its 'interests' against foreign intrusion or subversion.

Liberals believe that a Nation consists of real people; people who vary widely in their capability to deal with all the issues of life in a complex industrial society. Yes, a nation exists to provide security for its citizens. But 'security' means not only the 'security' of our borders and our business interests; it also means the 'security' of our environment, and the health and financial 'security', and the maximizing of economic opportunity, for the individuals that make up our Nation.

2. RELIGION—
Conservatives tend to be more religious; they trust God, and obey God. Conservatives reject the philosophy of secular humanism. To Conservatives, the Ten Commandments, along with Christ's teachings in the New Testament, are the proper bases of all law and behavior. Conservatives tend to accept the doctrine of 'original sin'. Conservative talk show hosts boast of praying.

Liberals tend to be secular humanists; they believe in the perfectibility of man, and in man's ability to guide his individual and social life by some version of the ancient, oft-stated, biblically-honored and universally-regarded Golden Rule. Liberals tend to reject the doctrine of 'original sin'.

3. THE WORK ETHIC—
Conservatives believe that everyone must make a contribution to society by working. No one ought to be rewarded for idleness, nor ought they be punished for success. Conservatives believe that all individuals, if allowed choices, are capa-

ble of providing for their own welfare and their own future through investments of time, money and energy. Conservatives believe that the pay for a job or position that is decided by the employer reflects the market value of that job or position, and is the end of society's obligation to that worker.

Liberals also believe in the 'work ethic', but are willing to cut a little more slack for those who lack the mental or physical skills to enjoy some of the common comforts of life that we've all come to expect in our country. Liberals believe that all working people, whatever their station in life or their particular talents, contribute to the general welfare of all of us, and deserve a small share of the overall success of the nation in addition to the pay they receive for their job.

4. CHOICES—

Conservatives recognize that they have some conflicting values about freedom of choice. They believe that individuals ought to be free to buy guns, but *not* drugs; they believe that people ought *not* have choice about abortion, but ought to have choice about schools and about their own 'social security'. Conservatives believe that government has an obligation to protect people from themselves; that since certain drugs can harm a person and may cause him to commit a crime, government has the duty to see that those certain drugs cannot be sold, bought or used.

Liberals are also conflicted. They believe that everyone is capable of making, and ought to be free to make, the decisions that affect his life so long as he does not harm another person. Liberals believe that government has no legitimate right to control personal behavior (e.g., drugs) that does not place others in imminent danger. And Liberals support choice regarding abortion. Yet Liberals also strongly oppose choice for schools and for a person to provide entirely for his own 'social security'. And most Liberals strongly oppose the personal possession of handguns.

5. PATRIOTISM—

Conservatives consider themselves 'patriots' because they believe in a very strong military and because they believe in personal freedom (to a point) and ostentatious display of the flag. Conservatives are also prideful because they believe in certain 'eternal verities'; i.e., The wisdom of the Founding Fathers, The Constitution as written, and the institution of Private Property.

Liberals tend to view patriotism a little differently. While they have the same love of country, and the same firm belief in our Constitution and in our democratic foundation and institutions, they also believe in constant challenging of the status quo to make our Nation a better place to live for more people.

6. GOVERNMENT—

Conservatives believe we can achieve more freedom and more personal opportunity with a smaller, less invasive and far less costly Federal Government. Conservatives believe that costs could be lowered and personal opportunities enhanced by privatizing—and thereby improving—many functions such as Schools, Parks, Public Lands and Social Security, and by reducing the number of regulations that hamper business activity. Conservatives believe the States must be given more responsibility over their own affairs

Liberals tend to have more faith in government as the operator of public facilities than they do in the private sector. They recognize the inherent inefficiencies and bureaucratic awkwardness of government-operated systems; but they seem willing to accept that penalty in the hope that such systems that serve the public at large will operate more in the interest of the general welfare than those systems that are geared to the profit motive.

7. PERSONAL RESPONSIBILITY—

Conservatives believe that Personal Responsibility, and Personal Rights as delineated in our Constitution, are two sides of the same coin for a healthy democratic republic.

Liberals agree; but Liberals also have created a reputation for themselves of not speaking out forcefully on the need for personal responsibility for one's actions. It seems that Liberals are always the folks who are looking for excuses or justifications for illegal or anti-social activities.

8. THE ECONOMY—

Conservatives believe that Capitalism, Free Markets and Free Trade are the best bases for producing wealth, and that the health and welfare of business must be favored over that of the individual in order to create new jobs and new wealth. Conservatives believe that prosperity must begin at the top of the economic scale and work its way through the system. Conservatives believe that wide disparity of incomes is a natural and healthy part of Capitalism because it creates incentive. Conservatives reject any deliberate re-distribution of wealth through the Tax System, or through other laws, such as Minimum Wage laws, that are designed solely to aid those of lower incomes.

Liberals agree with Conservatives that Capitalism, Free Markets and Free Trade are efficient at creating new wealth; but they also believe that the increasing leverage over the political process through the progressive accumulation of wealth and power into fewer and fewer hands, without any offsetting influences, becomes self-feeding and gradually introduces un-natural distortions into income distribution and political power. Liberals believe that general prosperity is maintained by assuring that continuous purchasing power is maintained at the lower end of the economic scale; that the economy will be stronger and healthier if measures are taken to assure that the purchasing power of ordinary people is enhanced beyond the levels that would occur through the untrammeled operation of capitalism and free markets.

9. LIFE—
Conservatives, generally being more tuned to a religious viewpoint, believe that all human life is sacred, and that life begins at the moment of conception; although there does not seem to be any clear substantiation for this view in the Bible. This belief, of course, requires them to oppose abortion because it's 'murder of the unborn'; but they can't seem to find the stomach or the logic to punish the mother for the murder. Paradoxically, however, Conservatives, generally, support the death penalty for any other crime of murder.

Conservatives believe that life ought to end only through the operation of natural processes of aging or disease. However, they *do* believe in using all the tools and knowledge of modern medicine to intervene in 'natural processes' in order to artificially prolong life. But they oppose any suggestion of self-inflicted suicide, assisted suicide, mercy killing or euthanasia.

Liberals, though largely secular, or nearly secular, and while disliking the ugliness of abortion, draw their tolerance for the act from the same Bible used by the opponents of abortion. Liberals can condone 'choice' because they believe that life begins, as God willed and defined it in Genesis 2:7, when the first breath is drawn and man acquires a 'soul'. To a Liberal, this is a clear metaphor that defines the beginning of 'life'.

10. HEALTH CARE—
Conservatives believe that any comprehensive system of taxpayer-supported health care for all citizens regardless of income or means is 'socialized medicine'. They say the Nation cannot afford it, and it will lead to a lower standard of care

and abuse of the system. In the minds of Conservatives, any 'national health care plan' is to be strenuously opposed.

Liberals, true to their philosophy of using government to share burdens and to enhance the financial security of individuals, favor some form of universal health care. Liberals feel that defending the health and body of every citizen against bacterial or viral invaders, and against debilitating disease, is every bit as important as educating every child and defending the shores or the skies against human invaders.

11. TAXATION—

Conservatives believe in abolishing the Income Tax and the system of Selective Entitlements in order to stop the invasion of privacy, the punishing of success, the corruption of legislatures and the hemorrhaging of our wealth.

Liberals are reluctant to give up the Income Tax in favor of any form of consumption tax because of the fear that the rich will not be paying a 'sufficient' share of the burden and that the poor will suffer.

12. TERM LIMITS—

Conservatives believe in Term Limits for all elected officials.

Liberals tend to believe that the voters in each election ought to have the choice as to whether to retain or throw out the incumbent.

13. CRIME AND PUNISHMENT—

Most Conservatives believe criminals must be forcefully punished, with the death penalty as a legitimate punishment for the most serious crimes as determined by law. Conservatives, generally, discount any 'heroic' attempts at rehabilitation.

Most Liberals are opposed to the death penalty, and most favor reasonable attempts at rehabilitation.

Goals, Objectives, Aspirations of Conservatives

What are Conservatives after? Where do they see this great Nation going? What do they want that Liberals don't want? What kind of a Nation do Conservatives want to see in the year 2050?

Conservatives have *not* liked what they see as the 'mushy' and 'confused' morals and the political, sexual and social mores of the American Nation of the last 50 years. They want clarity. They want guidelines based on Judeo-Christian values. They trust God.

Most Conservatives believe any sexual activity outside of the marriage contract is wrong. They believe that abortion is equivalent to murder, and they oppose assisted suicide. They're agreeable, but uneasy, with the acceptance of homosexuals as having all the rights and privileges of other citizens.

Conservatives want more social control (except for guns). They want laissez-faire Capitalism (the race goes to the swiftest). They want lower taxes and smaller government. They oppose a 'Progressive' Tax System, the Minimum Wage, Welfare, Social Security and any other 'redistribution of wealth' schemes under whatever guise. They want full voucher payments for choice of private or church-operated K-12 schools. They believe that government ought not do anything for people that people can do for themselves. They believe that all the 'liberal' social and economic programs of the last 70 years have failed and ought to be repealed.

In the macro-economy, Conservatives believe that growth is stimulated primarily by 'trickle down', by entrepreneurship, and by savings and investment rather than by consumer spending.

We've taken an author's license to itemize the aspirations of Conservatives for the next half-century:

1. To preserve the integrity of the United States of America and honor the values expressed in the Constitution.
2. To restore sound moral values to our Nation by enhancing Judeo-Christian influence in governmental institutions. By Conservative instincts, our rights flow from the Creator, and the foundation of all moral law is the Judeo-Christian Bible.
3. To confirm the sanctity of life; beginning with conception.
4. To confirm the concept of personal responsibility for one's actions, and to initiate tort reform to achieve this.
5. To minimize the size and influence of the Federal Government, and enhance Local control.
6. To assure Conservative control of the media and all three branches of the Federal Government.

7. To maximize the operational freedom of Capitalism and Free Markets.

8. To maximize the opportunity for individual accumulation of wealth, and oppose any redistribution of income or wealth through the tax system

◆   ◆   ◆

Now that you've finished the serious and provocative parts of this book, you're entitled to ask, "OK, now just what are the benefits from the Triad of 'Concepts' that Don and Lois are suggesting?"

How about a short list:

A More Moral Society	Longer and More Durable Marriages
More Security	Stronger Kids from More Stay-at-Home Moms
More Tranquility	More Fun
More Prosperity	Less Stress
More Personal Opportunity	More Time for Families

AS A GREAT NATION, WE CAN DO BETTER!

PART III
MUSINGS

6

SIXTEEN IDEAS TO UNSETTLE YOU

◆

SOME UNCOMMON COMMON SENSE
(As long as we've shaken your thinking by suggesting new styles of governing ourselves, let's see if we can shake it some more. Let's do some debunking, and some imagining.)

—ON SOCIAL SECURITY and MEDICARE, GOVERNMENT WASTE; FEDERAL GOVERNMENT 'TRUST FUNDS'; The FEDERAL RESERVE BOARD; ENVIRONMENTAL COSTS; GLOBAL WARMING; SCIENCE; HISTORY; SAVING MONEY; 10-year PROJECTIONS; The INCOME TAX; MALE SEXUALITY; POLITICS; ECONOMICS; UNIVERSAL NATIONAL SERVICE; and EVIL, VIOLENCE and WAR.

ENCOMPASSING MISTAKES IN THINKING BY BOTH MAN AND GOD.

1. SOCIAL SECURITY, MEDICARE—

You think Social Security and Medicare are in danger of going broke?

We're hearing vigorous debate on the possibility of Social Security, and Medicare 'going broke' by 2014, 2030 or some other vague date in the future. Both sides of the debate are either way out of touch, or are deliberately misleading. There's no more likelihood, or even possibility, of Social Security or Medicare 'going broke' than there is that the Defense Department or the Commerce Department or the White House will 'go broke'. Can't happen, won't happen, no way.

First thing to get straight—there is no 'pot' of money for Social Security, never has been! (At best, all there is is a stack of U.S. Government Bonds that have been purchased by the Social Security Administration. These are merely a promise by the Federal Government to pay back the money they 'borrowed' from the SSA.) This is exactly like you borrowing money from one pocket to put in another pocket, no difference.

Second thing to get straight—There's no magic in the stock market. Unless the true inherent value of any company increases with time, the increases in the value of its stock goes only to the lucky or successfully-manipulating trader. Unless the productivity of American industry were to improve proportionally with that extra invested capital that's diverted from the FICA, it's a fantasy to say that the ordinary investing senior is going to 'do better in the stock market'. The ability of the 'system' to support the growing 'senior' percentage of the population depends solely on the growth of productivity. Whether we cast our lot with a total 'government' program, or on the growth of the *real* value of the stock market, the requirement is the same; increasing productivity per man-hour of the work force. The alarmist folks who push 'Privatization' because '—by 2040, there'll be only 2 workers per retired person—' are missing the point. The answer is *not* in inflating share prices artificially by throwing new capital willy-nilly at the 'market'. Inflated share prices are not real national wealth. *Real* new wealth is created only by using human labor more efficiently through the application of energy, innovation and mechanization. All else is phantom.

There is no assurance that simply diverting worker's spare capital into the stock market won't simply inflate stock prices and create a bubble as happened in the 90's. The surest way to create new value over time is to end the FICA entirely, or invert[1] it, and allow a portion of that money to go into consumption of goods and services. This new consumption pattern would immediately put new money (investment capital) into the hands of those companies who are most efficient and effective at satisfying consumer demand.

Would this change sap the purchasing power of the higher-income earners? Of course it would; but there are two offsetting factors:
1. There are far fewer people earning over $65,000/yr., so the negative effect on overall purchasing of ordinary goods and services would be minimal.

2. The extra purchasing power of the lower-income earners would stimulate the economy to the extent that the movers-and-shakers who already earn over $65,000/yr. would find their total earnings and their returns on investment increased.

◆   ◆   ◆

The money that current recipients of Social Security are getting comes entirely from the ability of the Federal Government to pay (by redeeming the Bonds) based on current revenues or outside borrowing.

There are only two fundamental requirements to be met to assure that the needs of the Senior Citizens of the year 2030 will be provided for:

A. That the work force and the infrastructure in the year 2030 can produce a surplus of goods and services over and above the needs of the *working* population of 2030.

B. That the working population of the year 2030, acting through the Congress, elects to commit resources to the Seniors of that time. If they elect *not* to commit, neither FICA, the 'Trust Fund' nor any other hocus-pocus will work. The Seniors of 2030 and beyond would then be out of luck, period; unless they have accumulated a lot of private funds. But, you know what?—that ain't gonna happen!

2. GOVERNMENT WASTE—

You think the Federal Government spends more than it needs to, and that your tax money is 'wasted'?

---

1.   An explanation about the inversion of FICA. Presently, the FICA of 14% is levied on the first $65,000 of a worker's pay. For a low-income worker earning $20,000/yr., this is a contribution of about $2.800/yr. or over $230/month; for a higher paid worker earning $40,000/yr. It's $460/month. These are life-changing amounts; a dinner out occasionally, a computer, a new refrigerator, a new car, even a new home, or perhaps some into personal savings or college tuition. Ah, but where would the money come from to fund Social Security, you ask. Good question. And you may have guessed where from the word 'inversion'. We would levy FICA only on incomes *over* $65,000/year. The rate would be lower, even though there are far fewer payers, because of the far higher incomes on which the FICA would be levied.

You're half right; government does spend more than it needs to. But that 'wasted' money, in one way or another, goes as wages and salaries to American citizens who spend it or invest it. That money fuels commerce and adds to the profit of the folks who sell products and services; it returns to the economy.

But, wait, you say; if there weren't 'waste' in government, our taxes would be lower, and we would have more to spend on ourselves or invest the surplus; thus providing the same 'fuel' for commerce. True, except for one caveat; the people who are now the recipients of 'wasted money' would then be on welfare, or the recipients of charity, or they would have to go to work in the private sector. They still have to live; I don't think we believe in machine-gunning down people on the street.

We must assume that the private sector operates efficiently; it now has all the employees it needs to produce the goods and services it sells. If the private sector were careless and hired more employees than it needs, it would raise the prices it must charge to achieve the same profits, or it would make less profit; thereby lowering stock prices. Do we want either of those outcomes? Probably not.

Then we need to ask ourselves: Do we want those thousands of government employees that would be released tomorrow if we ended 'waste' in government to be on the welfare rolls or down at the missions begging for charity. Probably not.

Perhaps the 'waste' in government is only the symbol of greatly improved productivity in our economic engine. Perhaps as each year goes by, we need fewer and fewer people actually 'producing' in order to satisfy our needs and our affordable 'wants'. In the year 1900, about 40% of our working population worked on farms to provide the food we needed; in 2000, 2% provide all the food we need and we're able to export surpluses.

Fancifully, what if we wake up one bright morning in the year 2100, and we find that because of robotics, technology, improved teaching methods, fire-proof buildings, indestructible products, and crime reduction and justice simplification with lie detection techniques, only 10% of our population is able to produce all the goods and services we need or want? What do we do? Will 90% of the population be on the dole, or will we take turns working 2 days per month?

But, back to the real world, we do have to contend, each in our own way, with the Libertarian argument: Libertarians believe that all taxes (with the exceptions of those Constitutionally permitted) are 'theft'; therefore, we have no right to 'steal' from one person to provide support for another. That, of course, in the Libertarian view, is what most taxation is all about—'stealing'.

3. TRUST FUNDS—

You think Federal Government 'Trust Funds' exist?

'Trust Funds' (as far as the Federal Government is concerned) are a sham. There are none. We had no 'Trust Fund' for war in 1941, and the country was poor, but when the Japanese attacked Pearl Harbor, guess what? We not only found an immediate way to finance the war, but we tripled our industrial production to meet the needs of the war. Federal Government 'Trust Funds', are simply book-keeping and political legerdemain. Fact is, this great Nation can do anything it has the will to do. It all depends on the actions of the Congress.

The Federal Government cannot 'save up' money for a 'rainy day' or for a 'future purpose' like individuals or companies do; there simply is no place to put the money. (There's no bank big enough or safe enough.) Tax revenues must either be spent on current needs or 'invested' in capital improvements. Interestingly, the costs of all Federal projects are 'expensed'; there are no 'depreciation schedules'. The Federal Government, acting through the guise of, and at the whims of, the chimerical Federal Reserve Board adds to, and subtracts money from, the econ-omy. The Feds can stimulate, discourage and allocate production of goods and services by the private sector through tax policies, regulations and selective spend-ing of taxed revenues. Production of consumer items cannot be 'saved' for future use; the only way adequate resources for future needs can be assured is through current policies that insure that our Nation will continue to refresh, and add to, our production capabilities.

4. The FEDERAL RESERVE BOARD—

You think Alan Greenspan is an essential genius?

Actually, who needs him? The much ballyhooed and watched FED function of encouraging interest rates up or down to 'control' the economy is unneeded. Money is a commodity like bread or automobiles. In a free economy, when the demand for money in circulation exceeds the supply, because of a growing popu-lation or growing economic activity, the cost of money (interest rates) will rise. Competition for lending will keep the rise within bounds; thus slowing excessive economic expansion. And, of course, the opposite is true; slowing economic growth will reduce the demand for money, and interest rates will drop.

Of course, the total money supply to the economy furnished by the Federal Government must be added to from time-to-time as the population increases and/or economic activity increases. But, heck, a computer can do this better than a pompous and double-talking, and deliberately opaque, Federal Reserve Board.

5. ENVIRONMENTAL 'COSTS'—

You think Environmental Protection and Improvement is costly to the economy?

Capitalists who ought to know better keep dragging their feet in benighted opposition to measures that improve the environment. They complain that the costs will damage the economy; they're still complaining about this even though the last 30 years of cleaning up and protecting the environment have coincided with some of the most dramatic overall economic gains ever.. It ought to be obvious that the intellectual stimulation and job creation that results from cleaning up and protecting the environment far offsets any so-called 'costs'. And the bonus, of course is an improvement in the quality of life; cleaner air, cleaner water, more beauty. And, after all, isn't the quality of life, and human happiness, what this whole struggle of existence is all about?

A classic example: In the beautiful Seattle area, Lake Washington is a priceless asset; for its awesome beauty and setting, for boating, for swimming. 40 years ago, the lake was almost lost; it was in danger of being permanently spoiled by the increasing run-off from development and from sewage spills. Action was taken, large sums were spent; now Lake Washington is enjoyable for all of the reasons and activities that have always made it a jewel. Quality of Life!

6. GLOBAL WARMING—

You think Global Warming is a serious matter?

Well, by all indications the world has warmed up by something less than 1 degree F. during the last century, and sea levels have risen about 7 inches due to melting glaciers and expansion of the warmer ocean waters. We have no reliable data on what happened to the climate during the 18th and 19th centuries. Even if we did, what conclusions could we draw? 300 years of data, even if it were reliable, is microscopic in terms of the ages involved in both macro—and micro-changes of climate; it would prove nothing. We are fairly sure that ice once covered much of northern Europe and the northern parts of North America. So what?

So, OK, we're still warming up from the Ice Age. Is our use of fossil fuels speeding up the warming? What part of what cycle of climatic change are we in? Nobody knows the answer to either question; there is disagreement among the scientific community because none of them knows for sure; we have nothing to compare with. But, opposition to the Kyoto Protocol not withstanding, it makes good common sense and good geo-political sense, and good economics, to reduce the use of fossil fuels and get our energy from the sun, the wind, the oceans, bio-mass or fuel cells.

But let's assume the worst; that the climate will continue to warm at the present rate for the next 100 years in spite of our best efforts. So what?

Warm weather crops can be grown further north, cool climates will become warmer, ocean levels will rise at the rate of 7 inches per century (1/16th of an inch per year), rainfall patterns will change (some areas will benefit, some will be hurt), migration patterns may change, and animal and insect life will be modified, and maybe a few other changes we can't now think of. (Remember 'the law of unintended consequences'?). Remember also that any significant changes in human life and habits will take place over two lifetimes and several generations. Remember also that technology will be hard at work all the while to make whatever modifications in our lifestyle that may be both appropriate and beneficial. And who knows what unexpected benefits may accrue to the whole human race because of warming?

7. SCIENCE—

You think all of 'Science' is important and is respectable as truth?

Everyone ought to respect science; science has brought inestimable benefits to the lot of humanity. It has conquered hunger in the sense that the world can now produce far more food than it consumes, even if the population continues to grow. (Every nation on the planet has the capability to feed its own people; it's only overpopulation or deficient or corrupt political systems that cause famines.) Medical science and biological research is bringing us longer and healthier lives, and is even enabling us to control the number of new lives we bring into the world. Scientific research in chemistry, electronics and materials, together with sophisticated mathematics, is enabling better and stronger products and structures at lower cost, and is allowing us to explore the near space of our own Solar System.

But we ought not get carried away; let's separate science from 'studies'. We need to be chary about accepting as fact the conclusions reached by astronomers, geologists, paleontologists, archeologists, psychologists, sociologists or the practitioners in any other field where the conclusions reached cannot be duplicated and proven in repeated tests that satisfy our senses of touch, see, hear, and smell.

Ages of fossils and rocks, distances to the outer reaches of the Universe, age of the Universe, the number of 'Universes' that may exist, the creation of a living cell; none of these can be proven or duplicated. We do not <u>know</u> that 'carbon-dating' is accurate beyond a few hundred years because we have no way to verify the rate of decay over a long period of time and under the conditions of the earth's climate and cosmic ray intensity that may have prevailed in other ages. We do not <u>know</u> that the speed of light is constant throughout the Universe(s).

What we observe through the Hubbell telescope no longer exists at that place we see it, if it exists at all. Our observations through the Hubbell telescope are of bodies thousands or millions of light years away, they no longer exist at the observed time and place; if they still exist. If the distant Universe(s) had all been destroyed or consumed or re-formed in some galactic reversion of the 'Big Bang, we will never know it.

Evolution of certain short-duration life forms can be observed and verified within the span of a human's life; that the process of 'evolution' *does* occur can be called a 'fact'. But the whole varying descriptions of how man and other complex life forms evolved from a single cell must still be called the 'Theories of Evolution', because there is no way to replicate the process to achieve proof.

Certainly all the 'educated' and formally-presented theories of the 'soft' sciences are interesting and even entertaining, but one ought not believe they are 'facts', or that they are relevant to the serious problems of life here and now.

8. HISTORY AND THE FUTURE—

You think History is important and relevant?

Yes, the history that left documents of unchallengeable origin and authenticity, and that we still honor, are very important; our Declaration of Independence and our Constitution are exquisite examples.

And the history made and documented by men and women still living is recent enough to be relevant to the problems and difficulties we face today. The experiences from the 1930's, the Second World War, the Cold War, the fall of the Soviet Union are examples.

All history is marvelous entertainment, and ought to be valued as such. The History Channel and the library shelves full of Homer and of Will and Ariel Durant will intrigue many generations, as they should. But the cliche's 'Those who ignore history are bound to repeat it' or its companion, 'Those who don't know history are bound to repeat its errors' are meaningless nonsense insofar as looking for help in resolving current quandaries. We have a whole galaxy of problems to solve today, but they are 'today's' problems. Versus even 100 years ago, much less 500 or 1000 years ago, we are a whole new set of people with new worries, new knowledge and new technologies. It's our world, we and our parents created it; it's up to us to deal with it. It's important to worry about the future, but if we deal squarely and intelligently with the present, the future will take care of itself.

We can all worry about the kind of world we are leaving for our children and grandchildren; all generations have, and we do. But it's more important to remember that whatever kind of world it may be, it will be their world; the world they grew up in and helped shape.

9. SAVING MONEY BY INDIVIDUALS; THE QUANDARY—

The 'Quandary' of saving money.

While individuals need to save money for a comfortable retirement, or for a 'rainy day', such saving (deferred consumption) is actually not productive for the national economy. Our Nation is no longer struggling in an economy of scarcity; the huge productive capabilities of our free-market capitalism have created, instead, an economy of abundance. The growth of our economy depends on vigorous consumer spending. This spending not only reinforces our production machinery by enhancing the profits that provide the money for capital investment, but by the nature of *how and where* people spend their money, signals are continually sent to industry of what goods or services people want, and obviously those signals are sent to companies that most effectively use capital.

Thus, to deprive working people of spending money by taxing them through the present FICA of 14% is counter-productive to the future economy's ability to support them in their old age.

10. 10-year PROJECTIONS—

Can they be serious?

Do those 'serious-minded' people in Washington, to whom we pay $120,000 to $400,000 a year, really expect us to believe that 10-year Economic Projections are at all meaningful. Or for that matter, useful or necessary?

Can you think of any 10-year period in our 215-year history when conditions at the end of that period were the same as at the beginning? We're a dynamic country with constantly evolving technology and fluctuating interest rates, and with interests and obligations all over the planet. We won't be the same country in 2012 that we are today. We'll have problems and opportunities we can't even imagine today. In 1993, could you have imagined the impact of the Internet and the War on Terror?

Bad enough that we have grown men and women in Congress and in the Executive Branch acting like children, arguing over the tricky details of how we're going to spend the national income, or what the deficit and/or debt will be 10 years from now; worse yet is that they treat us like believing children.

It's a stretch to have confidence in the budget for next year; it's almost a lie to forecast 2 years ahead. Seems to us that, as in all human affairs, if we plan and act wisely in the present, the future will take care of itself.

11. The INCOME TAX—

An unimaginable boondoggle!

Yes, truly unimaginable. If one were to sit down with a clean sheet of paper and draw up a plan to get money to pay for the costs of government, it would be hard to imagine a more senseless or difficult way to do it than to tax personal incomes. Hard to imagine a more complicated, expensive, invasive, politically-corrupting and counter-productive way of extracting money from the economy.

To examine complex tax returns from 140 million taxpayers in exquisite detail is in itself an impossible nightmare. To require 140 million people to accumulate all the necessary detail to sit down and prepare returns, or pay someone else to do it, is unconscionable. For government to prepare and mail 140 million 100-page books to each taxpayer is a mind-boggling bureaucratic exercise and expense. To invade every home with a piece of paper that requires a report of every detail of their financial life is completely unacceptable in a free society.

Imagine the temptation to corruption and influence-peddling that's offered to every lawmaker to incorporate exceptions and interpretations in the regulations for special interests and situations. Actually, you don't have to imagine it; we have a 7500-page Tax Code to prove it already exists.

And can you dream up a better way to discourage initiative, creativity and hard work than to skim off the fruits of those valuable traits in increasing percentages? What better way is there to punish success?

1. How do you determine what constitutes income? Is it all the money that comes in from whatever source? What if I sell my car because I no longer need it? What are expenses; and do I get to deduct them before I report my 'income'? Which ones?

If I'm a business, I get to deduct *all* of my normal costs of operations, before I report my income; but if I'm just a working guy raising a family, I don't get to deduct *any* of the normal costs of *my* operations (food, clothing, shelter, transportation, utilities, credit card interest) before I report my income.

2. Now try to imagine the cost to both the government and the taxpayers of operating such a stuttering and incomprehensible system. Again, you need not imagine it; the cost to both the government, to administer, and to the private economy to comply, is a staggering $50 billion dollars a year. That's $357 per family.

12. POLITICS—

Most of the American people are 'lefties'; politically speaking!

(Left, means encouraging the vital Capitalist Free-market system, incorporating only the degree of regulation and legislation necessary to moderate destructive excesses. Left, means using government when appropriate to lubricate the machinery of production, and to extend the hand of community to those left behind. Left, means love of people and country. Left means a willingness to use force to combat evil. Left, means self-reliance, achievement and individual dignity. Left means maximizing personal freedom.

Left believes that using the resources of pooled effort can improve the lives of all. Within these meanings, virtually all Americans are on the political 'left'.)

We've talked politics to a lot of people in all parts of the country. Big surprise; they kinda' like things the way they are! Even those folks who say they're Republicans don't want the kind of country that the Republican Party of today wants to rollback to. Today's young turk Republicans in the House, Senate and the White House, you see, would really like to undo all of the legislation that was initiated under FDR in the 1930's and added to in the 40's, 50's, 60's and even the into the 70's by both Democratic and moderate Republican administrations and Congress'.

A lot of people like to say they're 'Republicans' because they associate the word with wealth, influence and a certain amount of cachet and sophistication; and, of course, they feel Republicans are more patriotic; these folks have a need to identify with the 'better people'. Democrats, you see, to them, are the hoi-polloi, the unwashed, the minorities, the unwise, the uninformed, the socialists (even closet communists), and, of course, Democrats are not *really* patriotic.

And, of course, the talk show hosts, (the Limbaugh's, the Hannity's, the Medved's, the Elder's, the Prager's, the 'Savage Nation's', the Hewitt's) the co-conspirators with, and handmaidens of, the new young turk Republicans, are engaged in a daily orgy of skewering and ridiculing 'liberals' in a kind of self-conscious and transparent attempt to appear oh-so-knowledgeable about the 'right' way to think. These talk show hosts have developed a pattern of setting up straw men from a crazy remark or action of an off-the-reservation nut so they can ridicule and sneer at 'liberals' in general. Little do they realize that not only is everybody onto their whole Tom DeLay-inspired conspiratorial and ridiculous games, but that all their listeners, except for a few right-wing nuts on *their* side who call in, are serious 'lefties'.

We haven't met anyone who wants to get rid of Social Security or Medicare, unless something better with the same security replaces them. The people don't seem to want to turn back the clock of progress. They seem content with those 'crazy' left-liberal programs like protecting the environment through the EPA, guaranteeing equal rights for minorities and women, protecting a woman's right to choose to continue a pregnancy, having a minimum wage law, protecting the rights of labor to organize, student loans, school lunches, Head Start, the Peace Corps, assuring pure food and drugs through the FDA, regulating the stock market through the SEC, conducting health research through the NIH, universal public education, National Parks and Monuments, Interstate Highways, wiring up the farms through the REA, guaranteeing bank deposits through the FDIC, and keeping a high 'wall of separation' between church and state. All of these seem a natural and acceptable part of life in a civilized and prosperous Nation such as ours.

13. ECONOMICS—

We've emerged out of the historic 'economy of scarcity'—

Historically, it has taken continual and back-breaking work to wrest enough sustenance from the earth to simply stay alive and support a family. The basic resources (land, air, water, minerals, forests) have always been abundant, but converting those resources into the survival needs of people has always required constant human labor. Gradually, as we learned to produce and use energy, we lessened the amount of human labor that was required to achieve the same output of goods and services needed for survival. Since human labor is the basic element of the 'cost' of everything, and costs, therefore, began to drop, we began to 'want' more of the goods and services available, and we began to experience 'leisure time'. But, of course, since 'needs' can be satisfied, but 'wants' never can, we were still faced with the necessity of allocating resources.

In the sense that our total means of production can now easily meet the reasonable 'needs' of all the people on the planet, we have emerged from an 'economy of scarcity' into an 'economy of abundance'. But there remain two problems:

1. We have organized ourselves into 'nations' with boundaries. Some of these nations have so developed their political systems, and have so perfected the means of production, that they easily produce, with minimal labor, all the goods and services their people 'need'. Other nations, with deficient political systems, have been unable to cope with even the 'needs' of their own people. And there's no real and practical reason why the folks in the prosperous nations ought to outright share their relative abundance with the folks who've not been diligent in seeing to their own welfare.

2. Within the prosperous nations, the production apparatus has become so proficient at satisfying 'needs' that it now becomes important to assure that the purchasing power of the general population is sufficient to satisfying 'wants' to the extent that the producers can maximize their profits. It does no one any long-

term good to create a new factory or means of production if there is insufficient consumption of product to keep the factory busy. This realization leads ineluctably to the conclusion that a means must be at hand to assure that personal income is distributed in such a way as to reward individual success handsomely, but still be widely enough distributed to maintain a high overall level of consumption.

14. UNIVERSAL NATIONAL SERVICE (UNS)—

One year for every young person!

This concept is an affront to the libertarian instincts in every one of us. And there's nothing in the Constitution to support the idea. But isn't it time to put it on the table for open discussion.

Upon graduation from high school, or upon reaching age 17-1/2 if not in high school, every young man and woman would be required to be part of the National Service for one year. The first portion of this service time would be a military-type of basic discipline and physical conditioning, the teaching of self-defense, and to familiarize young people with the care and handling of weapons. The remainder of the year's service would be spent in the continuing military or various tasks related to the construction and upkeep of the nation's infrastructure and park systems. About 4,000,000 young people would be rotated through such a program every year.

Granted that the cost of such a program would be huge, and the logistics of it staggeringly complicated; we can do it. As an example, during World War II, our Nation had only one-half the present population, and no computers, faxes, copiers or high-speed transportation and communications; yet within the space of 3-1/2 years, we inducted, trained and armed 12 million people. And even with all of those people taken out of the civilian work force, we not only fed, housed and supplied medical care to them, we built tens of thousands of planes, tanks, trucks, ships and billions of rounds of ammunition, that enabled them to defeat our enemies. In fact, in just the period from late 1941 to mid-1945, with 8% of our population, our most vigorous young people, out of the work force, this Nation tripled its industrial output.

A larger problem than the sheer logistics is what to do about the young people who become addicted to drugs at an early age, and the unwed girls who have children; or the increasing number of teen-agers who are obese or who have serious health problems. And, there's the serious consideration that many young people might intentionally resort to drugs or pregnancy to avoid the National Service.

Fortunately, our Nation has hundreds of thousands of talented professionals to help us cope with the problems of Universal National Service, and the rewards of UNS to both individuals and the Nation would be tangible and measurable.

15. MALE SEXUALITY—

The Intelligent Designer's big mistake!

To this point, we've described and detailed some mistaken thinking by you and me, and all the other humans in our country. But, God himself made at least one huge mistake, too. He created in the male human an unreasonably and unnecessarily intense sex drive; a hyperdrive that's slowly, but ineluctably, destroying us and our planet. So, we're about to have a talk with God—

◆   ◆   ◆

This whole mess wasn't necessary, God. We'd have done fine in populating the earth if you had endowed men with only the reasonable attitude toward sex that you saw fit to give to women. Sex is a fun activity, God; we'd have fooled around enough to enjoy ourselves, and in the process we'd have made plenty of children to please you and to assure our care in our older years.

As it is now, God, you've created many problems for the human community—

Because of the rampaging sexuality of the human male, and his inability to control it, we're damaging ourselves by producing too many new people and putting pressure on our life support systems and on our social interactions. Because of this incredible sex drive you created, men are imposing themselves on women, and on other men, indiscriminately and spreading diseases that cause untold miseries all over your world.

Even worse; because of this intense sex drive you instilled in men, they're raping and killing women and children in crazed attempts to satisfy their instincts for both sex and power.

Thus, we come to perhaps the most appalling aspect of the sex 'overdrive' of the human male; the lust for power! (And, of course, the lust for money is only a manifestation of the lust for power.) Yes, God, this lust for power over other people is the cause of all the war, killing, stealing and misery in your world; and the bearer of most of this lust is the testosterone-laden human male. Because, God, most of this 'lust for power' translates from the desire of every young and middle-age human male (though most males in our 'civilized society' won't admit this) to have untrammeled and unfettered access to as many women as he's able to service.

Why, God? Speaking for humanity at large; why did you do this to us? It's important for you to know, God, that many of us are trying our best with laws and customs to live within the boundaries of decency. We're trying our best to civilize and to improve our conditions. We've instituted marriage, and we're trying, against impossible odds, to uphold a standard of monogamy. We've passed many laws against the improper and destructive uses of sex. But it's a struggle you could have helped us avoid had you been a better planner and a more 'Intelligent Designer'.

16. EVIL, VIOLENCE and WAR—

It's OK to hate evil; and war and violence are sometimes essential—

In fact, pacifism in the face of evil is, in itself, evil.

While we don't believe that the inner nature of 98% of the human community is bad, there are in the world evil people, and there are systems that create and harbor evil and tempt good and decent people into their degraded circle. Civilization could not have advanced to the point that it has were most of the people in the world bad people.

While it is true that not all societies, groups, sects, etc. share the same values and mores for personal self-behavior, nearly all contemporary societies do recognize that it's wrong to physically harm someone else except in self-defense or to prevent a greater crime.

The Golden Rule—*Do To and For Others That Which You Would Want Done To and For You*—is a fair candidate for a universal code of moral behavior. Seems to be a guide for all the personal circumstances one can imagine.

Since the Ten Commandments (Exodus 20: 3-17) contain four (4) religion-explicit prohibitions, but are woefully inadequate and incomplete in describing the many kinds of acts which all civilized societies find to be both repugnant and criminal, they are not a proper posting for school classrooms; additionally, they're misleading for what they *don't* say. For example, a strict reading of the Ten Commandments would *not* tell a school child, or an adult for that matter, that one ought:

To Honor and Care for a Child (as one is exhorted to honor his father and mother)—
To Be a Good Husband or Wife—<u>Not</u> Beat One's Spouse

To Work Productively—
To Try to Make the World a Better Place
To Be Vigorous in Punishing Evil
<u>Not</u> Punch Out One's Neighbor—
<u>Not</u> Poison the Creator's Environment—

◆   ◆   ◆

Violence in punishing individual evil, or in crushing an inherently evil society is often necessary and is not to be foresworn. Pacifism in the face of evil is itself evil, and isn't holy.

War, as ugly as it is to conduct, is often the only road to peace and a better life. It is, indeed, a tragic experience to bear a child, then raise him for 18 long years with all the heartache, anguish, worry, expense and sacrifice, love and joy involved, then put him in a uniform and teach him to kill someone else's son, or to be killed. It is so important to be sure that war is, in fact, the only sane course to take to destroy evil. We have in modern precision weapons ways to wage war that need not result in such massive destruction and loss of life as in London, Dresden, Hiroshima or Tokyo.

The present policy of our government of not assassinating heads-of-state is outdated, cruel and wrong. To announce to those nations with whom we are at war, or who represent a clear and present danger requiring pre-emptive strikes, or who are committing unacceptable atrocities or genocide within their own country that we will refrain from assassinating their leader is self-defeating and is totally and unacceptably wasteful of human life.

True democracies do not go to war against each other, nor do they destroy their own people; therefore, the head of state of an offending country with whom we evaluate war as a tragic but essential option is an unelected tyrant and deserves death in any least destructive way we can manage it. If precise assassination is not possible, then air strikes to take out the center of government and other command and control centers after a leaflet warning to civilians are a legitimate option.

In any cruel, threatening or warlike nation, there are hundreds of people surrounding the leader who equally culpable and assisting him in carrying out his nefarious work. They know what they're doing, and their lives are equally expendable.

ABOUT THE AUTHORS

Over 61 years ago, in the early years of World War II, Don and Lois were two kids growing up about a city block away from each other in the seaside town of Santa Monica, California.

Don was a skinny 15-year old on a bicycle; he was courting Lois, a strikingly pretty blonde 14-year old, who's now a strikingly pretty blonde 75-year old. Both of us were raised in very ordinary working-class homes.

We dated through high school, though Don had lots of competition for Lois' favors. After graduation in June of 1944, it was the US Navy; in 1946, we were married in the Little Chapel of the Dawn at 20th St. and Arizona Ave. in our home town of Santa Monica. It lasted! 57 years later, we're still married; and even more remarkably, we're still good friends.

We brought into the world three fine people, Stephen 56, Gail 53 and Donna 44; they, in turn have added to our world seven beautiful and promising grand-children ranging in age from 4 to 22. We're traditionalists to the core; we believe in goodness, marriage, family, hard work and achievement.

Don has spent his entire professional life in the telecommunications business, beginning work as a young engineer in 1946. With 9 U.S. and Canadian Patents to his credit over the years, he established several world-wide and permanent changes in the design of products used for splicing and terminating telephone cables. For the last half of his adult life, he has worked actively in the world of political and social issues. He has conducted Discussion Groups for UCLA, he ran for the California State Assembly in 1974, and in 1994 ran for a City Council position in Rancho Mirage, California. As long ago as 1974, the 'New Guard' magazine published his article on tax reform.

Currently, Don is conducting a number of Discussion Groups in his community, and, with a co-host, has a weekly TV program, The CUTTING EDGE, in his home area where the pungent and inflammatory side of the issues of Religion, Politics, Sex and Morality are hotly and provocatively debated.

Lois has been a constant, challenging and equal partner with Don in our consistent struggle to understand, clarify and define ways in which we all might leave a better world.

The good life we've enjoyed, and the hope that the world of the 21st Century will provide an equally good life for our 'children' and grandchildren, has urged on both of us the desire to add value and substance to the country that nurtured and protected us. Our goal is to reduce the size and influence of government in our lives, and enhance the power, the security, the importance and the dignity of the individual, especially those individuals who work long, hard and tediously, but have lesser capabilities to climb the ladder of achievement. We emphasize the need to improve the lives of the working poor because the structure of our great Nation will always generously reward, as it should, the talented and energetic.

Quite simply, what Lois and I want is a Nation of more security and more happiness for more people.

This book is the result.

0-595-27534-6